TAKING THE FIELD

BY THE SAME AUTHOR

The Baseball Talmud

TAKING THE FIELD

A Fan's Quest to Run the Team He Loves

Howard Megdal

BLOOMSBURY

New York   Berlin   London   Sydney

Published by Bloomsbury USA, New York

All papers used by Bloomsbury USA are natural, recyclable products made
from wood grown in well-managed forests. The manufacturing processes
conform to the environmental regulations of the country of origin.

LIBRARY OF CONGRESS CATALOGING-IN-PUBLICATION DATA HAS BEEN APPLIED FOR.

ISBN: 978-1-60819-579-4

First U.S. Edition 2011

1   3   5   7   9   10   8   6   4   2

Typeset by Westchester Book Group
Printed in the U.S.A. by Quad/Graphics, Fairfield, Pennsylvania

To Mirabelle, a five-tool baby, and Rachel,
the Tom Seaver of wives.
I'll never trade either of you.

CONTENTS

AUTHOR'S NOTE

I use OPS+ and ERA+ throughout the text. OPS+ is, simply, on-base percentage plus slugging percentage, but normalized to reflect effects of that player's era (in 1968, offense was far scarcer than in 1998) and home ballpark (hitting in Coors Field is much easier than hitting in PETCO Park). A rating of 100 is average; above 100 is above average.

The same is true for ERA+ in terms of park and era, only with earned run average instead of OPS. Incidentally, an ERA+ above 100 is also above average.

TAKING THE FIELD

Chapter 1

WE ARE THE FANS WE'VE
BEEN WAITING FOR

IN RETROSPECT, all the years I didn't run for general manager of the New York Mets seem absurd.

It was strange to think of myself, a father, an adult, wishing so fervently for my team to improve and not having the courage to do anything about it. I wondered how I could have lived so long with this urge for a championship while never once asking myself what *I* could do. But leave those matters aside for a moment. Where did this call to public service, my campaign to become GM of the baseball team I'd reported on for much of my adult life (and loved since age six), come from? Not from a single place, or a lone idea, or one particular time the Mets made a decision that led to the unique heartbreak of baseball, spread unequally over 162 games with a payoff of sorrow at season's end.

It began in many places. I started my run for GM on trips to my father's office as a child. Asked to draw a picture while he worked, writing briefs and making calls, I'd draw a mock-up of Shea Stadium, placing names and statistics at the various positions, listing the starting staff on the mound and adding bullpen names like Franco, Innis, and Musselman beyond the crayon-built left-field wall.

I also began to run for GM during dark winter nights, laptop open, looking to reverse the fortunes of my favorite ballclub into the future. I filled the void of the off-season with a program called Baseball Mogul, which allows you to take control of a baseball team in any year from 1901 to the present, simulating games, making roster changes, and winning imaginary championships.

Sometimes this tool would let me reach into the past instead, taking control of the Dwight Gooden/Darryl Strawberry Mets and keeping them out of trouble, or wresting the reins from M. Donald Grant in the 1970s, giving Shea Stadium an offense to go along with stellar starting pitching and, most important: never trading Tom Seaver or Nolan Ryan.

But I think the need to run for general manager manifested itself when I began to think of the effect the Mets were having on my loved ones. Back in 2006, a year before I began to cover the Mets, my wife, Rachel, and I were ordinary spectators for Game 7 of the National League Championship Series. We'd managed to score tickets in the uppermost reaches of Shea Stadium's left-field stands, our view of the field partially obstructed—indeed, we only heard Endy Chavez's epic catch in front of the AIG sign. A brief silence befitting a backbreaking home run gave way to as thunderous a response as Shea ever emitted.

Of course, we know now that the Mets had only delayed their expiration—at the time, Endy's catch seemed like an omen. But for Rachel, who attended more games in 2006 than she had in her life previous to that, the joy experienced from her single year of true fandom gave me new perspective on what it meant to love a team.

And worse, in the parking lot after that game, this sport, described by the great A. Bartlett Giamatti as a game designed to break your heart, made my wife cry.

That is what baseball means to those who are lucky enough to follow it. It isn't merely a sport. Baseball takes hold of your life in a way that no other pursuit can. The schedule guarantees you 162 games a year at roughly three hours a pop—and on some nights, gloriously more.

And for the baseball fan, this is merely entry-level obsession. Hours and hours are spent talking about the game, reading about the game, shopping for merchandise to properly express love for the game, dreaming about the game. (Yes, I frequently have dreams in which I see the Mets choose to bring the wrong reliever into a tight eighth-inning situation.)

Look at it this way: The world expects us to love our mothers. But if we spent the same amount of time in conversation with our mothers, reading about them, wearing T-shirts with their pictures—we'd be institutionalized.

I think it was the birth of my daughter that truly illuminated the need for me to internalize this level of engagement and led me to the only possible response to it: running for general manager of the New York Mets. From the moment of her birth, even before it, I'd strategized the many ways I'd share the gift of baseball with her. But a different question presented itself as I recalled the many disappointments I'd experienced as a Mets fan: Exactly how good would the baseball I shared with her be? And what could I do to make it better?

The last few years have not been kind to New York Mets fans. Astoundingly, that 2006 season, which ended with Carlos Beltran striking out with the bat on his shoulder, costing the

Mets a trip to the World Series in front of a jam-packed Shea Stadium, was the best year we've had in a decade.

Those familiar with the team need not hear these grisly details. A 2007 collapse, losing a seven-game lead with seventeen games to play. An encore in 2008, a three-and-a-half-game lead blown with seventeen to play. (What a poor tribute to Keith Hernandez, whose number 17 will be retired once I am in charge.) A 2009 with injuries that made the Black Death seem tame. Only one in three Europeans died from the plague (33 percent), while twenty of the twenty-five Mets on the opening-day roster spent time on the disabled list (80 percent).

Despite this recent run, there wasn't any question as to which New York team my daughter would root for—the Yankees simply were not an option. Teaching her to tie her fortunes to a team that spends far more money than any other in baseball, entering each season expecting to be served a championship without putting in any investment, would run counter to everything we want to teach her about life.

Nor would either side of the family abide it. My father was a Brooklyn Dodgers fan before becoming true to the orange and blue. And I heard about the Holocaust before I heard about the Dodgers leaving Brooklyn—clearly, he thought I could handle the former at a younger age.

My wife's family was of New York Giants stock before joining the Mets cause. Her maternal grandfather suffered from Alzheimer's disease late in life but remembered two things right until the end: He was a Democrat, and he hated the New York Yankees.

So it was Mets or bust for little Mirabelle, and that raised the question: Shouldn't "Mets or bust" be a choice?

She would, soon enough, begin to follow the box scores as

I did, though probably not in the newspaper on the kitchen table but by computer instead. She'd find her favorite players, listen to the games, watch the games, and begin to talk baseball with me. I wanted her to smile when she did so. I wanted more happy recaps for my little girl.

It shouldn't be the way it was for me growing up. I remember arguing with my father on the way home from the grocery store one childhood night that the 1993 Mets would challenge for the National League East title. As long as Butch Huskey and Ryan Thompson reinforced Eddie Murray and Bobby Bonilla in the lineup, and Frank Tanana regained his 1980s form, the team had no holes. So I told him that night.

The 1993 Mets finished 59–103. And they only finished that well because of a season-ending six-game winning streak. I was heartbroken.

But that was a long time ago, and I've spent a lot of time learning about baseball since then. And during that time, I began to second-guess Mets decisions even as they happened. And really, if I believed that I was capable of making better decisions, in real time, on a regular basis than the Mets did, what other conclusion was there? Wasn't it my responsibility to the team? Wasn't it my responsibility to my daughter? It would have been negligent not to seek a popular mandate to become the next general manager of the New York Mets.

Think of the lengths we go to as parents to get our children into the best schools. Waiting lists for preschool, often tens of thousands of dollars for private institutions, and hundreds of thousands toward a college education that half the time won't land you a job. Most people are done with school by the time they're twenty-five, but our baseball team stays with us to our deathbeds.

And you can overcome terrible schooling. Lord knows I did. But I still haven't made my peace with the failures of the New York Mets.

It doesn't have to be this way for Mirabelle. It shouldn't be this way for Mirabelle. There's nothing about the Mets that suggests that two world championships and only a handful of playoff appearances need to be the result for the next fifty years, as they've been for the team's first half century.

While I mentioned that my wife has come to care about the fortunes of the Mets almost as much as I do, I'd be lying if I said she felt this way before we met. Rachel enjoyed baseball in the twenty-five years she lived before we began dating, but in a reasonable, emotionally balanced way. She'd root for the home team, and if they didn't win, it was a shame—the way forgetting a coupon is a shame, not the way poverty in America is a shame.

Our first date came on October 15, 2004, and we got engaged on April 15, 2005. Was it a coincidence that our courtship was completed over the course of a single off-season, the only conceivable period when my baseball addiction could be kept hidden? Many of my friends didn't think so. I'm not quite sure myself. In any event, Rachel received some early signs that could have tipped her off.

Early January, 2005: Rachel and I returned to her apartment following a lovely evening of dinner and a movie. This being early times, I reluctantly asked her if we could watch ESPN News, and she happily complied.

In the bottom right-hand corner, a countdown clock ticked toward zeros. I explained that Carlos Beltran was perhaps the best all-around player in baseball, a center fielder who could field his position remarkably well, hit tons of home runs, steal bases at a ridiculously high clip, and would immediately become the best player at the position the Mets had ever had. I did not explain what the clock meant, which must have been bewildering to her.

Finally we reached midnight. I jumped off the couch, pumped my fist, and yelled out, "All right!"—a response to sports-based success I learned from my father—and Rachel tried to understand well enough to celebrate with me.

"So Beltran is a Met now?" she asked, gamely.

"Well, no, not yet."

"So then what did the clock mean?"

"Well," I said, returning to what could be described as my senses, "that was the deadline for the Astros to offer Beltran salary arbitration. Now that they haven't, they won't be able to sign him until May first, meaning he'll almost certainly be signing elsewhere."

"So we just sat watching a clock to find out who Beltran won't play for?"

Well, yes. But this was a breakthrough moment for us: Rachel had asked this incredulously, but without malice. We hadn't watched a game together since we'd started dating, but it was the beginning of a pattern: She always respected the intensity of my feelings for the New York Mets, and she knew that my need to see every game, discuss the team, and write about them extended beyond simply a professional imperative.

The night we got engaged, the Mets and Marlins battled at early-season Shea Stadium. For one of the few times in my life, I actually gave away my tickets to a Mets game to friends, and proposed on the beach in Cape May, New Jersey, the state's southern tip. After the fortuitous answer, we returned to our hotel room to call friends. Naturally, I thought the friends I had at Shea Stadium would want to be the first to know.

When I reached them, I was shocked to hear that Aaron Heilman had pitched a complete-game one-hitter. Of course, the Mets have never thrown a no-hitter in their forty-nine-year history.

Between phone calls, I told Rachel about Heilman's feat and the Met curse. Certainly I believed the Met victory on the night of our engagement provided a positive omen. But if we'd missed the first no-hitter? Would that have been a sign from the cosmos that I'd made a huge mistake?

These thoughts have been calmed, mostly by the Mets' 5–0 record on our wedding day and subsequent anniversaries, but also, to a lesser extent, by a happy and rewarding marriage.

I think it was a small moment that really crystallized for Rachel how much the Mets mattered to me. Late in August 2005, the Mets took on the Phillies, trailing them in the wild-card race by just one and a half games. In the eighth inning, walks to David Wright and Victor Diaz brought Ramon Castro (more on him later) to the plate with the Mets trailing, 4–3.

I was watching from our apartment bedroom, a cat on each side of me, Rachel periodically entering to check on the game. She happened to be walking through the door when Castro launched a long home run. I pumped my fist wildly, sending both cats sprawling and landing me on the floor. Rachel rushed over to see if I'd hurt myself, but I was on the carpet, laughing, the broadcast still ringing throughout the room. After several years of mediocrity, the Mets looked to be contenders again.

"You really care about the Mets, don't you?" Rachel asked. She knew, intellectually. But you can't fully understand it until you live with a baseball fan through a season. And yes, I really care about the Mets.

It is that joy, the feeling of falling off the bed because of a three-run homer, that I want to bring to my team. It is the pursuit of that unique euphoria available only to those who experience 162 games, then still more in the playoffs, with the payoff of all that invested intellectual energy and psychological trauma—perhaps beyond any other experience life has to offer aside from marriage and childbirth.

In fact, not all marriages or childbirths. It takes a spectacular marriage filled with communication, mutual understanding, and ludicrously fantastic sex to compete with the average baseball season. Meanwhile, test scores clearly indicate fewer and fewer children can live up to any Mets season, let alone 1969.

There are, of course, a few rare seasons that measure up to those great partnerships, and they seem to rise up from nowhere. Take, for instance, the great Mets season of 1969, the gold standard, when every bit of the joy came as a complete surprise. But a careful look at how that team was built will make it seem as if a championship was never in doubt.

Chapter 2

A CALL TO ARMS:
BUILDING THE 1969 METS

M Y DAUGHTER WILL never experience a 1969 Mets
season. I don't simply mean that in the literal, chronological sense, either. Unless she abandons the family team for
some not-yet-imagined expansion squad, she will never know
what it is like to root for a team that has nothing in its history
but massive losses. That kind of future is hard to contemplate.

In all likelihood, the 1969 Mets will be to her what they were
to me: a magical breakthrough in the history of my team but
one emotionally elusive to me. For those who lived it, like my
father, it felt as if the logic that the world rested on had been
entirely upended.

It must have come like a bolt from the blue (and orange):
Out of the ten teams then in the National League, the Mets
had finished either ninth or tenth in each season from 1962 to
1968. But there are misconceptions galore about this team, from
the idea that only picking Tom Seaver out of a hat made the
World Series possible to the mistaken notion that this team
greatly overachieved its talent.

In reality, the 1969 Mets were a carefully built team that

shrewdly combined the products of a fantastic farm system with trades to fill the areas that the system hadn't stocked. And while this team, created in the forgotten era before free agency, didn't have the advantages latter-day Mets teams would enjoy, the lessons to take from the assembly of the 1969 team are many. And like any serious candidate for the unelected office of general manager, I have made it my business to learn them.

Taking apart the reasoning behind how the roster was built provides the best indication of how to evaluate individual talent for a championship team.

Bing Devine, the man most responsible for the rise of the Miracle Mets, came to New York only after getting fired by his hometown team and lifelong employer, the St. Louis Cardinals. St. Louis stood six and a half games out of first place in August 1964 when Devine, a former executive of the year, got the ax. By the time the Cardinals rallied to win the 1964 World Series, Devine had been snapped up by the Mets.

Also critical to the team's success at that time were Johnny Murphy, who oversaw player development and became GM in 1968, and Whitey Herzog, who served as director of player development beginning in 1967. The trio's successes were overwhelming; later, the loss of all three in a short span spelled the end of the Mets' success.

The three men, as the rest of this chapter will make clear, all focused heavily on the farm system. Before free agency, this was the only way to build a baseball team. And it's not surprising that men like them are needed again now: As free agency has evolved, more teams have found ways to lock up their best players during their peak seasons, or to trade those players—for prospects—before they become available to everyone.

In other words, player development is arguably even more

important for the Mets now than it was in the mid-1960s, since a strong farm system is required to produce the prospects to trade for high-priced stars that a New York team can afford, but are signed or traded before they reach the free-agent market.

But of course it mattered a great deal in the 1960s, too.

To the history books, then. Who, my daughter will briefly wonder, were the '69 Mets? Let's start with the everyday players. Remember, the amateur draft went into effect in 1965, so the Mets were free to sign young players at will in 1962, 1963, and 1964. In 1963, they signed left fielder Cleon Jones, who would later hit .340 in that magical season and catch the final out of the World Series. Shortstop Bud Harrelson also signed in 1963, as did right fielder Ron Swoboda.

Cleon Jones is best known in my family as the reason my father almost won a sucker law-school bet. A classmate of his rooted for the Pittsburgh Pirates, led at the time by Hall of Fame outfielder Roberto Clemente. While Jones was a strong hitter for average, with a career .281 mark during a pitcher-friendly time, Clemente blew him away: He won four batting titles, hitting .317 for his career. Still, my father bet that Jones would have the higher batting average in 1969.

But in 1969, Jones battled Clemente to the wire. Jones actually led with three games to go, but Clemente went 7 for 13 over the season's final weekend to improve his average to .345, just a few points higher. An undisclosed amount of money was forked over. It would not be the last time my father lost money betting on the Mets.

The point is less about whether Jones was the equal of Clemente—he wasn't—and more about what the 1969 Mets made people feel. By that time in his career, Clemente was already a likely Hall of Famer, while Jones, barely twenty-six years old, had never so much as hit .300. But that team made a knowledgeable baseball fan like my dad feel that, just for a while, the rules didn't apply. In 1969, Cleon Jones could outhit Roberto Clemente.

What is historically interesting about Jones, though, is that he was one of the few Mets for whom '69 was a career year. Both Harrelson and Swoboda checked in right around their career averages. Again, this team was no fluke.

The Mets also drafted regular second baseman Ken Boswell in the fourth round of the 1965 draft, which meant that half the starting lineup came through the Mets' farm system. More fun still for those rooting for them: Not a single everyday player checked in above age twenty-six. Swoboda's platoon partner, Art Shamsky, was the old man at twenty-seven.

There's a lesson in that—both in terms of New York's ability to embrace unproven young players, and also in trusting young players to be pleasant surprises. In today's star-hungry off-seasons, we often ignore the reality that, much of the time, veteran players either stay the same or get worse. (Hello, Jason Bay; hello and good-bye, Vince Coleman; Jim Fregosi, we hardly knew ye.) With youth, very often, the reverse is true.

The genius of that team extended well beyond the simple scout-draft-develop-repeat formula. Catcher Jerry Grote is a good example of how the Mets seemed to steal talent at that time.

Grote had been with the Houston Colt .45s (renamed the Astros in 1965), and in 1965 enjoyed a strong year at Triple-A. His so-called "slash stats" (the three most important indicators of good hitting, which I use throughout this book: batting average/on-base percentage/slugging percentage) were .265/.344/.420. From a twenty-two-year-old catcher, this would be considered impressive by today's offensive standards, let alone in the far more pitching-friendly 1960s. Grote also had world-class defensive abilities. And he had a roadblock named John Bateman.

Bateman hit a far more impressive .297/.330/.586 for Triple-A Oklahoma City, leaving little doubt whom Houston would start at catcher in 1966. The decision provided immediate payoff for Houston, too: Bateman hit .279/.315/.467 in 1966, despite playing half his games in the pitcher's haven known as the Astrodome.

So finding a match with the Astros made sense. The Mets dealt Tom Parsons, a promising starter, to Houston for Grote. Houston was pitching starved, and the Mets had better pitchers ready to take Parsons's spot, anyway. He never pitched in the major leagues for the Astros, while Grote played a dozen seasons in New York and made two All-Star teams.

Again, here is a perfect example: Fans may think, during the off-season, that they care about marquee names, but if a team starts to win, the fans will fall in love with anyone. I remember my father telling me about Jerry Grote, about his cannon arm, about his ability to gun down runners. The Mets knew they had something special in Grote back in 1968, when he caught all twenty-four innings of a 1–0 loss to Houston, throwing out the only two runners who tried to steal on him—one in the twentieth inning, the other in the twenty-first. Great players create these memories for us. And too many of my memories are of Todd Hundley dropping fly balls in left field, or Mackey Sasser failing to throw the ball back to the pitcher.

Third baseman Wayne Garrett spent 1969 on the Mets, in part because he had to. He'd been selected in the Rule V draft out of the Milwaukee Braves' system. The Rule V draft allows other teams to pick a player who has been in the minor leagues for a certain period of time but has not made it onto the big-league roster. The rule, like the amateur draft, was aimed at preventing teams (the Yankees, really) from stockpiling all the young talent.

Garrett possessed a tremendous glove at third base, and posted a .625 OPS (on-base plus slugging, about which see the author's note for more) in Double-A, which at the time was relatively strong for a twenty-year-old. He didn't hit much in 1969, but his strong defense made him valuable, and he started to hit better by 1970. It was the type of high-upside acquisition that paid off in the long term, and it helped a surprising amount in the short term as well.

It is impossible to think of the 1969 Mets without Donn Clendenon, whose home run in Game 5 of the World Series helped start the Mets' comeback, and whose shots in games 2 and 4 were ultimately the decisive run in each. The road to Donn Clendenon, the first baseman and World Series MVP, ran through four prospects: Bill Carden, Dave Colon, Kevin Collins, and Steve Renko. Of the four, only Collins and Renko played major-league ball, and only Renko enjoyed any extended success.

But the Mets didn't deal for Clendenon until June 15, 1969. That he was the final piece of a championship team makes trading four prospects for a thirty-three-year-old first baseman understandable. (Though one wonders how it would be received if it happened today.) Moreover, Renko, at other moments in Mets history, would have been untradeable—either for legitimate reasons (a lack of other young pitching options) or for more dubious ones (too much time spent selling the fans on the limitless future of . . . Steve Renko).

In other words, having Gary Gentry, Nolan Ryan, Tom Seaver, Jerry Koosman, Tug McGraw, and others come through the farm system is what allows a team the luxury of dealing a Steve Renko.

So let's do some totaling up here: For seven everyday players on a World Series team—Grote, Clendenon, Boswell, Harrelson, Garrett, Jones, and Swoboda—the Mets gave up five prospects, only one of whom amounted to anything. The one draft pick, Ken Boswell, was a fourth-round pick. In other words, little in the way of outgoing talent was required of the Mets to assemble the overwhelming majority of their lineup.

It is perhaps most impressive, however, to examine how they acquired the final everyday player in the 1969 lineup: center fielder Tommie Agee.

Clinically, the acquisition of Agee buttressed the 1969 Mets in key areas. An intelligent baseball executive acquires a player like Tommie Agee to have, in one package, a plus defensive center fielder, a power hitter, a leadoff hitter, and a stolen base threat. To a Mets fan, the imminent danger of a leadoff home run—Agee totaled 26 long balls while hitting from the top spot in the batting order—a stolen base, or a breathtaking catch is the reward. In Game 3 of the 1969 World Series, Agee provided two of them, first ranging far into left-center field, then managing the same feat while chasing a ball down against the fence in right-center field. He sprinted across the outfield, diving on the dirt of the warning track to make the game-saving catch—twice. This was almost exactly three months after Neil Armstrong walked on the moon. Who displayed greater range? Meanwhile Agee had also led off the game with a home run.

Agee came to the Mets along with backup infielder Al Weis

after the 1967 season in exchange for four players. Two of them, Buddy Booker and Billy Wynne, played only briefly. The other two were Jack Fisher, a starting pitcher, and Tommy Davis, whose impressive performance in 1967 was, at the time, the best offensive season any Met had ever enjoyed.

But Davis had already begun to break down. He'd played 154 games in 1967 at age twenty-eight, but had played in a total of only 117 in 1965 and 1966, and he played only one full season from 1968 to 1974.

Fisher, meanwhile, was the essence of mediocrity as a starting pitcher, and already twenty-eight as well. He pitched reasonably well in 1968 for Chicago, but was out of baseball by 1970.

Agee's 1967 hadn't been as strong as his 1966, but he'd still managed to post above-average offense in center field while providing one of the best gloves in the American League at the position. Most important, Agee was just turning twenty-five. This was the kind of forward-thinking acquisition that folks like Billy Beane are beloved for today.

One other element worth noting here: Agee was terrible for much of the 1968 season, and the Mets did not give up on him. They knew that his terrific years of 1966 and 1967 meant far more than the down year he experienced in '68. This was because of his age, talents, and previous track record. Needless to say, his work from 1969 to 1971 vindicated their faith in him. (All this is borne out by today's sophisticated metrics, such as OPS+; Agee's good years provided a much more meaningful sample than the one bad one he had.)

So, where does all this leave us? What lessons are here for a fan, a team, or a would-be general manager?

The first is the need to spend as much money on player development as possible. To this day, the huge majority of countries are not subject to baseball's amateur draft, making international talents (for instance, Felix Hernandez) available to the highest bidder. Meanwhile, simply offering large bonuses to players considered difficult to sign allows large-market teams to snap up first-round talent in the later rounds. For example, the Yankees drafted Austin Jackson, a talented high school outfielder, in the eighth round of the 2006 MLB draft. He'd fallen that far because he'd committed to playing basketball for Georgia Tech. But the Yankees offered him $800,000—far more than an eighth-round pick usually receives—to play baseball instead. When Jackson agreed, the Yankees acquired a first-round talent with their eighth-round pick. It's that simple.

For the Mets to spend so much on major-league salaries while languishing near the bottom in spending on the draft means an organization perpetually lacking in young, inexpensive talent—precipitating the need to overspend on the major-league roster, leaving less money to spend on the draft. And the vicious cycle continues. Winning organizations not only acquire talent but generate it, and the Mets have done so consistently only twice in their history—winning a World Series each time.

There are other themes here that emerge from a good fan's study of Mets history: not relying on a player to repeat an anomalously successful season, staffing the team with young players to both optimize health and allow the development curve to work to your advantage, identifying surplus talent in another organization to help a weak spot within your own, and making decisions that help your organization in the long term, enjoying any short-term success along the way as a bonus. When there's a plan, the fans will come along for the ride. The Mets finished no worse than third in the National League in attendance from 1964 to 1968. This is a lesson we'll return to, both when the Mets have been patient, with positive consequences, and impetuous, with disastrous ones.

But one can only learn so much from the story of Bing Devine and his position players. As the 2010 Giants teach us, you can go a long way with homegrown pitching, even if your lineup is . . . uninspired. And, really, what good were the '69 Mets without their pitching? Take a look at these résumés from the 1968 Mets organization:

In Triple-A, the Mets had a pitcher, at age twenty-two, who had 50 strikeouts and just 8 walks over 53 innings. A pair of twenty-six-year-old starters posted ERAs of 2.97 and 3.51, respectively. A twenty-four-year-old struck out 56 in 61 innings, with a 2.07 ERA. At Double-A, a twenty-one-year-old starter pitched to a 2.41 ERA in 168 innings, striking out 142. Another twenty-two-year-old starter pitched to a 3.12 ERA, striking out 107 in 156 innings. A twenty-one-year-old had a 3.38 ERA as a swingman. A twenty-four-year-old posted a 1.56 ERA with 63 strikeouts in 75 innings. And another twenty-one-year-old swingman had the most impressive season of the above lot, with a 1.75 ERA over 138 innings, striking out 120.

What do these pitchers have in common? None of them were Nolan Ryan, Tom Seaver, Jerry Koosman, Gary Gentry, Jim McAndrew, Tug McGraw, or even Steve Renko. Most of them you've never heard of. (In order, they are Larry Bearnarth, Bill Connors, Danny Frisella, Don Shaw, Jim Bethke, Rich Folkers,

Bill Hepler, Dennis Musgraves, and Barry Raziano.) The point is, the late-1960s New York Mets had *that* many pitching prospects.

Where did they come from? Hepler was a Rule V acquisition; Bethke, Musgraves, and Bearnarth were amateur free agents; Folkers, Raziano, Frisella, and Shaw were all acquired in the draft. Connors was purchased from the Chicago Cubs in 1967. The Mets had plenty of pitching prospects by then. But they understood they couldn't have enough.

And the pitchers who threw more than 71 percent of the innings on a pitching staff considered one of the finest in major-league history? Koosman and McGraw were amateur free-agent signings, as was Seaver.

We all know what it feels like to watch a great pitching phenom—in retrospect. This past summer, I considered taking my daughter to Washington, D.C., so she could see Stephen Strasburg. By the time she could make the trip, an elbow injury had sidelined him.

Really, we don't know about any one pitcher. Not Strasburg, nor Mark Prior, nor the number-one pick in the 1994 draft, Paul Wilson. You need to stockpile, and twenty years from now, my daughter can brag about the one phenom she saw—and won't bother talking about the five she experienced before injuries took their toll.

But luck isn't everything. Consider the following story when evaluating just how lucky the Mets were in the case of Seaver, and how much their luck was the residue, as Branch Rickey put it, of design.

The Braves had drafted Seaver but signed him to a contract for a $50,000 bonus after the college baseball season had started. The commissioner's office voided the contract, but then the NCAA ruled Seaver ineligible. In an effort to find Seaver a home, the commissioner said that any team willing to pay Seaver that $50,000 bonus could participate in a hat pick. Only three teams stepped forward: the Phillies, the Indians, and the Mets.

In other words, the Mets' best hope was a one-in-three shot. But seventeen out of the twenty teams at the time—85 percent of the league—couldn't have gotten Seaver with all the luck in the world. They didn't give themselves the chance.

Gentry, McAndrew, and Ryan were all draft picks, although it's noteworthy that none of them were blue-chippers. Gentry went in the third round, McAndrew in the eleventh round, and Ryan in the twelfth. (Author's note: *The twelfth round!*)

Contrast that with the current Met spending on draft picks, generally: thirtieth in baseball in 2009, twenty-fifth in baseball in 2010. It isn't any wonder that the team lacks the pitching prospects any organization craves.

In other words, the 1969 Mets, despite the lowest possible expectations, did exactly what it took to build a championship team, making themselves inevitable. The recent-vintage Mets, despite the highest possible expectations, have managed to do everything necessary to avoid acquiring the very reinforcements they've needed.

And yes, that '69 team had tremendous pitching—but the fans, like my father, fell hard for the position players, too. Mets fans loved Cleon Jones, who hit for average, Ron Swoboda, who hit for power, and Bud Harrelson and Jerry Grote, who didn't hit much at all but could field their positions well.

Mets fans didn't need a team with a theme. They just wanted to embrace a team that won. That's all any of us want. And the Amazin' Mets, it seems, weren't a miracle after all: They were proof that you can have that success if you follow some basic rules. Of course, there are more modern techniques to incorporate as well, all of which I began to touch on when I formally announced my campaign in June 2010.

Chapter 3

MORNING IN AMERICA

"This team can't even lose when it's supposed to."
—RACHEL MEGDAL, JUNE 18, 2010

CONSIDER THIS: When I first decided to run for general manager of the New York Mets, most of my opposition came from people questioning why I'd want to change things up on a winning team. These arguments came from people who should have known better, should have understood the difference between a streak and a winning season, and who could not see, as I did, the deep structural flaws in the way the New York Mets operated.

But it is easy to get caught up in the small moments of a baseball season. (In fact, I'd even say it's essential.) A two-week stretch is usually about twelve games—in the scheme of a season, it's almost meaningless. But think about how long two weeks feels in your life. When your favorite team does nothing but lose for that long, it feels as if you'll never see them win again. And when they win for that long, even levelheaded individuals start to wonder if all the calculations, all the little details we'd been obsessing over, were nothing more than simple analytical errors.

Who you gonna believe? The facts or your lyin' eyes?

As a fan, it was a surreal experience for me, seeing the Mets climb above .500 in June and challenge for the division lead with a roster teeming with flaws. Under normal circumstances, I would've been circumspect, but still giddy, to see the Mets still in the race as spring turned to summer. But this year things were unusually complicated. I knew I'd have a more receptive audience for my campaign if the Mets lost more than they won. But I'd have happily sacrificed my general manager ambitions for the chance to see playoff baseball come to Flushing. And as much as I wanted to be GM—quite a lot—there was no point to any of it if I couldn't enjoy watching the Mets win.

When I really asked myself what I wanted, it was to be in the stands with my family during Mets games, in the clubhouse before and after, and describing the entire experience with the distance that being a writer and fan allows. To do the general manager's job right would mean seeing much less of my wife and daughter than suited me, to give up working from home, to excise completely the remaining fun that existed in baseball. Covering the team had been both a job and pleasure. But tasked with the responsibilities of running my favorite team, I knew I could never rest.

So if this year's Mets managed to win the pennant . . . how would it feel?

Lousy. It would be a mirage. One I'd celebrate with my family, watch recordings of for years to come, but one that would do tremendous long-term damage to the organization. They'd receive confirmation that making decisions ad hoc pays off.

Sure, teams get lucky for a season all the time. A few players excel, some others have unexpected breakout years, or a few veterans rally for a last hurrah. (See the 2010 San Francisco

Giants for details.) But I knew these Mets, and they simply weren't on a path to sustainable success. They were on a path to riding some stars and hoping they got lucky with the rest of the team.

And throughout Omar Minaya's tenure, especially as it wore on, the Mets didn't get lucky—quite the contrary.

But 2010 wasn't simply about luck changing. Although my wife was in her third trimester at the time, I was the seemingly hormonal one at the dinner table on January 22 when the Mets paid the Angels $2 million and gave up Brian Stokes for the right to take on Gary Matthews Jr. Not only had Matthews ceased to be a viable major leaguer three years before, but he played center field, creating a roadblock to simply starting Angel Pagan, arguably the team's best player, at his natural position.

Or who could forget when the Mets signed Mike Jacobs on February 11, a player who'd been nontendered by the Royals. *Mike Jacobs?* This choice felt especially significant for a personal reason.

Back in 2005, my wife and I had been enjoying a sun-kissed afternoon at Shea Stadium, no less beautiful despite the 7–0 lead Kris Benson had staked to the Washington Nationals. With two on, a longtime minor leaguer named Mike Jacobs came to the plate for the Mets to make his major-league debut. An instant later, he'd deposited a ball in the seats, the first bit of good baseball news of the day. Rachel had just excused herself to go to the restroom.

Jacobs had a ridiculous rest of 2005—11 home runs in 100 at-bats, driving up his trade value so much that he became the centerpiece for acquiring Carlos Delgado. And as Jacobs faced the Mets in subsequent years, every time he came up, Rachel would remember, "That's the guy who homers every time I go to the bathroom."

So when the Mets brought him back—this relic of my courtship of my wife—I should have been overjoyed. But I wasn't, and not because I'd soured on Rachel. I didn't want the Mets employing a first baseman with a wooden glove and a .698 OPS. Something told me he'd be in the opening-day lineup. That something seemed abstract and nagging at first, but later it turned out to be Jerry Manuel, who scheduled him to hit cleanup.

It didn't go well.

Within a few weeks, the Mets disposed of Matthews after just 65 plate appearances, releasing him outright and eating the money they'd paid him. They jettisoned Jacobs after just 28 at-bats. He was paid $900,000 for his services.

I liked seeing the Mets learn so quickly from their mistakes, but it was disturbing to consider that their opinions of both players were a) clearly wrong and b) tenuous enough that they could reverse course on them after less than a month. What if Jacobs had hit .400 in his first 28 at-bats? What if Matthews had hit 6 homers? Would the Mets have locked them both into the starting lineup? The former Met Mike Cameron once hit 4 homers in a single game—would the Mets have assumed he'd be good for that every night?

It happened with Guillermo Mota. The Mets had acquired Mota in August 2006 for absolutely nothing from the Cleveland Indians. At the time, Mota's ERA was an unsightly 6.21, after he'd posted a miserable 4.70 ERA the season before. But Mota pitched to a 1.00 ERA in 18 regular-season innings over the remainder of the 2006 season. Buoyed by the small sample, manager Willie Randolph used Mota in high-leverage situations throughout the playoffs (though his form quickly reverted), and continually went to him throughout 2007 despite his 5.76 ERA. It is hardly a stretch to say that Randolph's reliance on Mota cost the 2007 Mets the division title—the team lost by a single game. And Randolph only had the chance to overuse the mediocre Mota because Omar Minaya signed him, on the strength of those 18 innings, to a two-year, $5 million contract.

So I worried a lot, and with good reason.

My favorite team didn't need better results—at least not immediately. It needed a better strategy. At a certain point, positive results only threatened to derail a change in how the team operated. If an alcoholic friend lands a great new job, your enthusiasm is tempered by the fact that he'll drink his way out of it in a few months.

And yet I couldn't root against my favorite team. I just couldn't. I was happy for every Jeff Francoeur single, not that there were many of them, even as I knew wasting his at-bats stood in the way of prospects who could help more in the long term. I took pleasure from the outs Pedro Feliciano recorded against right-handed hitters, even as I knew Jerry Manuel's use of him in such spots would be deadly over the long term. And certainly I couldn't help but love the story of R. A. Dickey, the thirty-five-year-old knuckleballer enjoying his first major-league success.

But as the team that had begun the season 18–20 improved to 43–32, those around me began to wonder if all this was simply part of a Mets plan finally coming to fruition.

For several weeks I'd been working on a detailed piece about the decline and fall of Omar Minaya for a publication's debut issue. As the debut drew nearer, the Mets went out and swept the Phillies, shutting out their vaunted hitters in all three games. They beat the Yankees two out of three, then swept the Marlins. Rod Barajas, the veteran catcher with a career high of 21 home runs, remained on a 50-homer pace.

My editor called me about a week before publication. "We need to change the focus of the piece," he said. He was as incredulous as I was. Do I need to mention that he's a Mets fan?

Instead, mixed among the writers talking up the miracle Mets, my debut piece discussed the Plan B Mets, how they were held together with duct tape, how continued success was unlikely.

This is perhaps the most distasteful part of my job—when I see the Mets having unsustainable success, I feel compelled to write about how unlikely it is to continue. As a fan, I want to believe otherwise. Instead, I hope against my own writing. Usually, the professional me wins out—when it comes to the Mets, anyway. (Don't get me started on the Yankees. Not yet.)

A couple of weeks later, my high-powered superagent, Sydelle Kramer, sent me an e-mail that said:

Hi Howard—

Don't know about you, but I keep waiting for the Mets to implode, and it still might happen—but it might not! Never thought I'd be writing those words.

Sydelle

This came from, arguably, the most rational person I know—and also the person who'd e-mailed me a few months earlier, worried about how little David Wright was smiling. Baseball does that to you.

And rooting for your team is an impossible habit to break. On Friday night, June 18, Hisanori Takahashi, a thirty-five-year-old with no previous major-league experience, threw six shutout innings to help the Mets top the Yankees. It was the eighth win in a row for the Mets, their longest streak in two years.

Even under normal circumstances, this was a surreal moment. Mets fans were optimistic, probably for the first time in several years. It was sudden and unexpected—and yet they were beating the top teams in the league. We also knew it might not last, but we couldn't admit it to ourselves.

Except for one tiny community of fans: the ones who were about to launch their campaign for GM. Population: me. And my wife, sort of. That was the public I'd be facing when I announced my run for general manager.

So I knew what this meant: No matter the case to be made for change, of long-term negligence and an uncertain future, I could be stepping in front of the cameras on Monday morning to declare that a Mets team that had just won ten in a row and swept the Yankees needed a new general manager.

Baseball sometimes does that to you, too.

It also can make people angry, or maybe serve as a channel for anger that would be better directed elsewhere. As someone whose writing ends up on the Internet, I knew this all too well.

After I wrote a piece for the *New York Observer* in August 2007 called "Chien-Ming Wang, Occasional Ace," predicting that the Yankee pitcher would have huge swings in performance due to the number of balls in play he allowed, several comments on the piece were written in Mandarin. After consulting with a friend, I discovered that these were death threats.

I was overjoyed! Rachel was frightened. But consider my side of things: I had written something that created such a visceral response across the globe. It was a thrill, and I truly believe to this day that the chances the writer would fly from Taiwan to New York to murder someone over the concept of defense-independent baseball statistics are extremely remote. (Besides, Chien Ming Wang's fans have bigger fish to fry these days. As of this writing, he's trying to keep a spot with the Washington Nationals.)

But there you had it. I was about to take the first major step in my public campaign: a press release. And let's just say the responses were not all favorable. Here's what I sent out to my colleagues, the bloggers who would become my delegates, and posted on my brand new Web site, Megdal forGM.com:

MEGDAL TO ANNOUNCE DECISION ON RUN FOR GENERAL MANAGER

MEGDAL TO MAKE INTENTIONS CLEAR AT MARRIOTT MARQUIS, ENDING SWIRLING SPECULATION A FEW FLOORS BELOW SWIRLING RESTAURANT

On Monday, June 14, at 11 A.M., Howard Megdal, writer for SNY.tv, MLBTradeRumors.com, New York Baseball Digest, and Poet Laureate of Amazin' Avenue, will reveal his decision concerning an electoral campaign to become the next general manager of the New York Mets. Mr. Megdal will make a statement and take questions from the media.

The event will begin promptly at 11 A.M. on the fourth floor of the Marriott Marquis, 1535 Broadway (at 45th Street). At the conclusion of the event, lunch will not be served.

Megdal, 30, would be making his first-ever run for general manager of the New York Mets. His career to date has included a wealth of relevant experience, however, including writing about the team for the *New York Observer*, authoring a definitive profile of Cowbellman, and finding several different rhyme schemes for the phrase "Big Pelf."

Megdal also understands the fan perspective. He is a Mets partial-season ticket holder, attended David Cone's 19 strikeout game on October 6, 1991, and served one day as a political prisoner over his love for the New York Mets during Phillies Hat Day at Beck Middle School in Cherry Hill, NJ.

WHAT: ANNOUNCEMENT/MEDIA AVAILABILITY BY
       HOWARD MEGDAL

WHEN: MONDAY, JUNE 14, 11 A.M.

WHERE: NEW YORK MARRIOTT MARQUIS, FOURTH FLOOR

Every bit of that press release was true. Naturally, some were receptive to my sense of humor—and some weren't.

My biggest surprise came from some who got the joke but feared it. After all: It *was* a joke, except that it wasn't. I didn't love my chances, and I intended to keep my sense of humor about it, but I had something to prove. In the same way my parents and grandparents viewed so many public figures through the lens of "good or bad for the Jews," there seemed to be a worry among some at Amazin' Avenue that my run for GM would delegitimize the entire stat-based movement.

The worry was a natural consequence of the years much of baseball's entrenched thinking had ridiculed and dismissed sabermetrics. But the fear of victimhood remained in a few long after this battle had been won in most quarters. So instead of considering that my elevation of these ideas could help make the Mets a better team, some members of the site were convinced the humor of the project would allow decision makers to reject all arguments without hearing them.

Or, as BobbyV_Incognito wrote, "Howard, I'm not questioning your ability, or your passion for the Mets, but something like this isn't going to make bloggers look good to the Mets management, or everyone else in general. Especially since the Mets are doing well so far."

Others were less charitable. Njk237 wrote, "If you want, I could probably find the time to work on a campaign poster for you in MS Paint. I'm fairly sure I could draw you with your head up your own ass."

And one member of the Amazin' Avenue staff with a clear sense of perspective even vowed to "put down and bury" the campaign, presumably with the help of the Taiwanese.

It's hard to explain how it felt to be berated like this. I wanted what they wanted: a winning team, making good decisions. I was willing to work for it. Sure, maybe it was a gimmick. But the rational arguments had been made on Amazin' Avenue, in my columns, and in the writing of others for years. A gimmick is designed to draw attention—but to ideas I took very seriously. We were talking about the Mets, and I am always serious about the Mets. And I was, I hoped, being good-natured about it.

The support came just as passionately, and in greater doses. Carleigh Ottwell, who writes the blog Lost in St. Louis, wrote:

> Let me preface this by saying that a baseball team is only as good as its players and what they do on the field. I will be the first person to say that. Despite this, there are people in charge for a reason. That is why I fully support and endorse Howard Megdal for GM of the New York Mets (visit MegdalforGM.com for more info). No, it is not an elected position, but he's a smart guy who has good ideas and wants to do what's best for the team, which in turn is really what's best for the fan base, and all involved. When he talks about making a decision, even in an imaginary situation, he has reasoning behind his ideas.

The writer King Kaufman sent his support via e-mail, since I came from Cherry Hill, New Jersey, and he once knew a girl from there. Other writers, like Rob Neyer, Dayn Perry, and Zoë Rice, wrote positive things about the idea. But it took Dana Brand, the Mets writer and Hofstra professor, to put the run in context:

> It looks to me as if Howard is trying to examine, with humor and quite a bit of subversive insight, the assumptions that underlie the whole system of baseball. Why is it that in modern America, where we're pretty much agreed that monarchies and dynasties aren't smart ways to run anything, we allow baseball, which means so much to so many of us, to be run as if it were the most primitive form of feudal aristocracy? What about our democratic values? Why does no one even advocate the idea that baseball should be run of the people, for the

people, and by the people? What would it be like if we lived in a world where our baseball leaders were as answerable to us as our political leaders are supposed to be? Howard poses this question, it seems to me, without being too obvious about it. I think this is very funny and very interesting. It's the kind of smart, wacky performance art baseball could use. It makes me wonder what it would be like if baseball fans had power, and if we didn't have to feel, so often, as if we were medieval peasants, passionately loyal serfs, with no power at all to affect our destinies.

How that would fare against Internet vitriol in the voting booth remained to be seen.

As we drove from our Rockland County home to the Marriott Marquis, I thought of my first trip into New York City. My parents and I had traveled north on the New Jersey Turnpike, through the Lincoln Tunnel, and as we exited into the light, the first thing we saw—that anyone saw—was Dwight Gooden, rearing back, prepared to throw that fastball or curveball that so many hitters missed for much of the 1980s.

Entering New York City had always been that for me—heading to the place where the Mets play. Never mind the difference between boroughs, Manhattan and Queens—what does that mean to a seven-year-old? New York is where the Mets play. And the Marriott Marquis is where we stayed during a vacation when I first fell in love with the city.

So it seemed only right that I booked my campaign announcement there, getting a discounted rate when I explained my project to the booking agent. Turns out he roots for the New York Mets, too. "Anything I can do to get Omar out of there," he said, and cut the rate in half.

I felt many things on that drive as I went over my speech. Certainly I felt a bit nervous—would the speech land, both with the live audience and, more important, with Mets fans viewing it on the Internet? Would my agenda be clear to those I hoped would support me?

Also, how exactly should I interact with people? On my right hand I wore one of those giant foam fingers you get at the stadium—a closed fist with the index finger pointing up: METS #1! Would people shake it? Could you glad-hand in such a thing?

Mostly I felt empowered. No longer was I simply sitting in the press box, or the Promenade, Section 508, or, before that, Section 7 at Shea Stadium. At last I could move beyond those who simply booed the team's misfortune, who despaired that nothing could ever change, and point the way instead to a better future for the New York Mets.

My call to action had been a loud one, its volume amplified by each move the New York Mets made (or failed to make). It was time to reach out to my fellow Mets fans and show them there was a better way.

I knew when I got home I'd tell Mirabelle, without exaggeration, that I had taken action to provide some of the most enduring memories of her childhood. This was no generic thought for me: My memories, as they related to the New York Mets, were very specific.

I turned six just before the 1986 baseball season—on the day pitchers and catchers reported, in fact. I think it is fair to wonder if my subsequent fealty to the game of baseball is due in some part to that first season. It was a magical, once-in-a-lifetime experience, happening to me in the first year that I'd ever really wanted it.

But the deepest emotional attachment to that season doesn't resonate with me when I think of Bill Buckner, or Bob Stanley's wild pitch, or even the tremendous sixteen-inning game that catapulted the Mets into the World Series.

The day most seared into my psyche is October 11, 1986. Game 3 of the National League Championship Series fell on a Saturday afternoon, and with my mother working, it was left to my father to take care of me for the day. That meant an afternoon of baseball, the Mets' first home playoff game in thirteen years.

Consider that for a moment. Between home playoff games by a team in the biggest market in the country, my father had moved to New Jersey, become a partner in a law firm, bought a house, raised a child for more than six and a half years, and seen four presidents serve. In 1973, Al Kaline, Hank Aaron, and Roberto Clemente were active players. In 1986, Barry Bonds, Roger Clemens, and Greg Maddux were active players.

I don't remember much about the game itself, though I've subsequently become fully versed in every twist and turn—the early Astro lead, the three-run homer from Darryl Strawberry to tie it, the 5–4 lead Houston took in the seventh, and, of course, Lenny Dykstra's heroic two-run home run to win the game. It was that last moment that I remember. My father, a reserved man, a respectable attorney, a grown adult, the man who taught me most everything I knew about the world—jumped off the sofa and did what he believed was the Mexican hat dance. Was it a real Mexican hat dance? These days I doubt my dad is an authority on the subject, or ever was. But he did it anyway. It involved an off-key singing of that familiar refrain from *Jarabe Tapatío*—"da-dum, da-dum, da-dada-dadum, da-dum!"—and

the pumping of a fist in conjunction with a kind of jump danc-
ing, as if our floor were a treadmill. But certainly it will always
be the Mexican hat dance to me.

In my memory, the scene then jumps to a walk with him
through the rows of on-sale books at the Camden County Public Library. The game had ended early enough for us to visit a
book sale—what a concept, major-league baseball, an afternoon
LCS game!—and I walked to the counter barely able to see over
the stack of books I'd found, every one of them about baseball.

Who could blame me? This magical sport had transformed
someone I was used to seeing speaking carefully into a Dicta-
phone about subclauses and parameters into . . . a very different character. And it had hooked me as well. By that infamous
Game 6, I remember racing off the bus (where the bus driver
had told me that the Astros held an early 3–0 lead) and stay-
ing glued to our television in the den, joined shortly after I
came home by my father, through every moment of that 7–6
marathon.

All this happened, of course, because the Mets were run
by Frank Cashen, the finest general manager in team history.
Those are the stakes for everyone who runs a major-league
baseball team. Either you are creating iconic childhood memories for children throughout your fan base, or you are consign-
ing those kids to long, sad winters that begin before August is
even through.

For my announcement speech, I wanted to let Mets fans
know, through broad themes, not only why I had undertaken
such a project but what I would do if given the job. A handful
of media members showed up to the press conference, which
is what I expected. After all, not a single beat reporter for a

major-league team believes he is less than the finest choice to become general manager—it is what drives them to analyze the team.

In other words, I was horning in on their territory, even if my success would pave the way for others. I couldn't say I was surprised: I knew it would take time to build my fan movement and draw the attention of the ESPNs of the world.

But I had to go for the gold from the very beginning. I channeled the greatest orators in American political life. If words had proven effective for Abe Lincoln, for Robert Kennedy, for Winston Churchill (and, though I did not know it at the time, for Christine O'Donnell), I felt similar sentiments could best capture the perilous state of my favorite baseball team.

I knew it would be important to present my ideas as seriously as possible. I fixed each media member with a purposeful stare as he shook hands with my orange foam novelty finger, then strode confidently to the podium and delivered my speech.

As Abe Lincoln said many years before becoming the sixteenth president of the United States, "I will study and get ready, and perhaps my chance will come." Today, for me, that moment is here.

Today I am announcing my candidacy for general manager of the New York Mets. I do not run for this position to oppose any man, but rather to propose new policies. I run because I am convinced that the Mets can become an organization governed by LOGIC, TRANSPARENCY, and PASSION, and, because I have such strong feelings about what must be done, I feel that I'm obliged to do all that I can.

I do not come to this decision lightly. I am extremely happy in my current vocation as a sportswriter. I get the opportunity to write about my favorite team for SNY, for New York Baseball Digest, and as Poet Laureate of Amazin' Avenue. I have written for MLBTradeRumors.com, ESPN .com, and the *New York Times*. I have been given the opportunity to discuss baseball with the very players who play it best, and the decision makers who shape the greatest of all sports.

But while I have written about the New York Mets for most of my adult life, I have lived and loved the Mets since I was six years old. It is the optimism the Mets provided me that year, 1986, that drives me to take on unlikely causes, to believe in the implausible. Mookie Wilson's ground ball, in other words, is what compels me to be here today.

I grew up in difficult circumstances, just fifteen minutes from Philadelphia, and as a result, spent much of my childhood surrounded by Phillies fans. When I was thirteen years old, my school principal forced me to spend the day in his office, since the school had declared Phillies Hat Day and I refused to remove my Starter pinstriped Mets cap. Had I agreed to remove the Mets hat, I would have been set free. But that was too high a price to pay.

I will never forget my first trip to New York, seeing the light shine down upon my family's car as we exited the Lincoln Tunnel, and there, standing over us, a perfect vision: Dwight Gooden, delivering a pitch. New York was, and should be, a National League city. A Mets city. An orange-and-blue city on a hill, whose citizens have cause to believe, cause to hope.

But for nearly fifty years, Mets fans have lived on hope alone—too often, success has been fleeting and easily avoidable failure has crushed our spirits. We take pleasure in the hot streaks of today, while the grand design flaws lead to losing streaks tomorrow. We have relied on the Magic to be back, for something Amazin', instead of trusting the often fickle baseball gods to turn our way due to a consistently well-constructed team.

In the coming months, I will work to earn the mandate of the fan base I call home. I will be running in primaries hosted at twenty of the most popular Mets blogs on the Internet. I will answer every question, put forward my agenda for the New York Mets, and hope to gain the support of the more than five million monthly readers at these twenty blogs.

These blogs run the gamut of approaches, from stat-heavy to scouting-intensive, reporter-based to fan outlets. Represented are professors and blue-collar Mets fans, some based in the Northeast, others spread out across the country. After all, those of us whose emotions are dictated by the rise and fall of the blue and orange aren't simply found in the five boroughs, in Rockland and Westchester, in Long Island, New Jersey, and Connecticut. We are everywhere.

And I invite fans of every team to join this crusade. Fans of the Indians and Reds, Royals and Athletics, Rangers and Twins, help to elect me and you will be doing more than just contributing to the success of the New York Mets. It is easy to lump all New York teams together, of course, to think of the Mets as the Yankees with less pretension and a nicer ballpark. But this simply isn't so.

New Yorkers themselves are desperate for a strong alternative to the Evil Empire. The Red Sox in recent years showed that the Yankees can sometimes be beaten. But Boston cannot siphon off a majority of New York's fans itself, leaving the Yankees without the very source of their financial advantage that allows them to treat the rest of baseball like, to quote a Steinbrenner, "the Toledo Mud Hens."

A balance of power in New York is to the advantage of every team in Major League Baseball. Let 2009 serve as a warning: An Iron Curtain is descending upon the game we love, and the World Series trophy will sit, year in and year out, within its barbed-wire boundaries.

New York was once a National League city. I believe it can be again, just as I believe it always will be when the Mets consistently give New Yorkers a reason to believe. And it is up to us, as Mets fans, to take control of our destiny, to build upon the battles won at Coogan's Bluff and in Flatbush and at Shea Stadium.

It is time to make the Yankees what they once were, what they should be forever more—New York's other team, with fans who express anger at anything less than a championship, and, upon winning a title, nothing more than relief. A team that doesn't even have the decency to play baseball by the rules. It is time to take our city back from the privileged few, from the malefactors of great Steinbrenner wealth.

It is a cause that calls for more than hope, however. Under my watch, the Mets will employ logic in personnel matters large and small. Players will be drafted, signed, or traded for with an eye on more than just tomorrow's headlines in the New York tabloids, or simply short-term success. After all, long after I complete my tenure as general manager, I will still be the same season ticket holder I am now, attending games with my parents, my wife, my daughter, and my friends.

A sustainable pipeline of players through careful drafting will supplement intelligently spent money on the very best free agents, and, yes, some of those prospects will be traded for in-their-prime stars. No more spending B-plus money on C-minus free agents, or failing to leverage New York money properly, watching the generous spending of the Wilpons wasted on overpriced mediocrities.

My administration will be one of transparency as well. I will not be perfect: Mistakes are a part of a game as complicated as baseball. It is why we love it. But I will not hesitate to acknowledge those mistakes, as Franklin Roosevelt put it, to admit them frankly and try another.

Mindful of the many Mets seasons that have been derailed due to an unexpected injury or a veteran fading at precisely the wrong time, as general manager I will make certain that every chance taken has a fallback plan as well. And I will tell you precisely why I am doing everything I do and hold myself accountable to questions about these moves, both from the press and, more important, from the fans.

I can appreciate that there is a certain audacity in this endeavor. And though no one has spent more time thinking about how to best make the New York Mets consistently excellent than I have, this is no cerebral exercise. I will wake up every day that I am general manager with one goal in mind: to make the New York Mets, the team so many of us think about every waking moment, the best possible ballclub on and off the field, now and in the future. Under my watch, no Mets employee will have any other mind-set than to let fans know that their passion is our passion. Why should you come to the ballpark, after all, if you believe you care more than the Mets do?

Let us join together in this endeavor, to take back the city of New York, to take back baseball itself, and deliver consistently effective management to the fans of the New York Mets, a fan base that has waited nearly a quarter century for a world championship and nearly fifty years for the kind of team that New York truly deserves. Smart but not smug. Successful but not soulless. A team that takes true joy from its successes and learns from its mistakes.

Under my watch, the Mets may not be champions every year. Baseball is, after all, a game designed to break your heart. But as Branch Rickey said, "Luck is the residue of design." And no move I make as general manager will happen without that grand design in place, without you, the fans, aware of how it fits, and without my complete emotional investment in making the choices I do.

To paraphrase John F. Kennedy, "Ich bin ein Mets fan." For those who don't speak German, that phrase literally translates as, "I am a Shake Shack Burger." But let us not lose sight of the larger point. I am you. In the coming months, you, the fans, have a chance to put me in a position to voice our preferences and discontent not just by cheering and booing, but in every decision, large and small, of the baseball team we all love so much.

I invite all who love the Mets, indeed all fans who love baseball, to join me in this cause to take back the game itself. Let us do more than simply cheer or boo—let us take direct control of the franchise that holds sway over our emotional well-being. Let us no longer simply be observers.

So let us begin anew. I do not shrink from this endeavor: I welcome it. The energy, the faith, the devotion that we bring to it will light up Citi Field and all who love it. And the glow from that fire can truly light the world.

And so, my fellow Mets fans, ask not what your baseball team can do for you; ask what you can do for your baseball team. My fellow fans of the baseball world, ask not what the Mets will do for you, but what together we can do for the freedom of all baseball-kind.

I knew the questions that followed wouldn't be easy ones, but what better time to start displaying what I felt was the proper way to explain oneself to the fans?

Ted Berg of SNY.tv, my editor, a longtime friend and suffering Mets fan since 1987, started in with the hard questions right away. He asked me about Oliver Perez.

Perez, for those unfamiliar, burst onto the scene as a twenty-two-year-old for the Pittsburgh Pirates in 2004, with a 2.98 ERA and 236 strikeouts in 198 innings. Stardom seemed to be his logical next step, but as baseball fans now know, Oliver Perez never does the logical thing.

In 2005, he managed to get an opening-day start, pitch to a 5.85 ERA, and get sent down to the minor leagues before the end of the season. In 2006, he had an ERA over 6 with the Pirates and well over 5 in Triple-A. Still, he was just twenty-four, with a fastball in the midnineties.

I still remember walking toward the elevator in our apartment building one evening about three weeks before the trade deadline in 2006. I said to Rachel, "You know who I'd like the Mets to trade for? Oliver Perez." I went on to explain his star-crossed journey, expressing faith in both Rick Peterson's ability to fix him (Peterson was then the Mets' pitching coach) and a belief that the Pirates screwed Perez up because, basically, they were the Pirates.

Rachel seemed amenable, provided I would still take her to dinner.

Three weeks later, the Mets experienced a twist of fate that would come to be considered Metsian in the subsequent few years. In the early-morning hours of July 31, the Mets' best relief pitcher, Duaner Sanchez, allegedly got hit by a drunk driver while out in a taxi after curfew in pursuit of a late-night meal. (At any rate, that was the team's story, and they've stuck to it.)

Suddenly, with the trade deadline a few hours away, the Mets lacked a setup man for Billy Wagner. This being Omar Minaya's Mets, a reasonable bullpen arm could not be found in Triple-A. (A minor leaguer named Heath Bell had struck out 11 batters per nine innings for Norfolk, the team's Triple-A club, but he was a nonprospect in the team's eyes. Now, of course, he is the elite closer for the San Diego Padres, the man who replaced Trevor Hoffman.)

Instead, the Mets traded their starting right fielder, Xavier Nady, for Roberto Hernandez, a forty-one-year-old former closer nearing the end of the line, and the enigmatic Perez.

Perez posted a 6.38 ERA in seven starts with the 2006 Mets, but I felt there was more to the story. He'd had two good starts in the playoffs, and his so-called "peripherals"—nontraditional stats that folks like me pay attention to—were very strong. For his 2007 campaign, I predicted 16 wins and an ERA between 3.50 and 3.70, for which I was roundly derided throughout the Internet.

By the end of the year, the derision disappeared. Perez pitched to 15 wins and a 3.56 ERA.

In 2008, the first month or two were difficult, but he sorted things out. Over the last five months of the season, he had a 3.56 ERA. For a pitcher known as inconsistent, that was remarkable consistency.

That winter, Perez hit free agency. To me, he represented many things to be valued. He was twenty-seven, meaning he was entering his prime. His fastball velocity had ticked up one mile per hour from 2006 to 2008, and his changeup had improved, giving him another pitch to go with his slider and his enigmatic "slow slider," which looked to most of us like a curveball. But I didn't worry about terminology—I just wanted Perez to stick around.

Few teams wanted to give him a long-term contract; I saw this not as a warning but an opportunity. The Mets were able to sign him for just three years, a short commitment by most standards. What it all meant was that the Mets were getting (so said I) the three best seasons in the career of a pitcher with a lot of strikeouts, a great fastball, no injury history, and two straight seasons of better than league-average pitching. At $12 million per season, they were paying a premium for his upside, but I wholeheartedly approved.

Needless to say, it didn't turn out well. In 2009, Perez had a 6.82 ERA over 66 innings, then had knee surgery to end his season early. In 2010, he pitched to a 6.80 ERA over $46\frac{1}{3}$ innings, missing part of the season with a recurrence of the knee problem surgery was supposed to correct.

As I was saying: Oliver Perez is consistent.

He refused a minor-league assignment despite his massive struggles and spent long weeks on the Mets' roster without getting the chance to pitch, due mainly to the horrific results whenever he did pitch.

Oh, and that fastball? He lost three miles per hour off of it. It may not sound like much, but . . . yeah. You get the picture.

The craziest part is, if I had it to do over again, I'd use the same measurements to evaluate a pitcher and I'd come to the same conclusion. A remarkably similar pitcher to Perez is Jonathan Sanchez of the San Francisco Giants. The two are near clones. Sanchez has a similar repertoire, he is also left-handed, his fastball velocity is nearly identical to Perez's in '07 and '08, his K rate and his walk rate all nearly the same. Even his build is comparable to Perez's.

Sanchez just completed his age-twenty-seven season for the Giants in 2010. He pitched to a 3.07 ERA, better than Matt Cain or Tim Lincecum, and struck out 205 in 193⅓ innings.

That should have been Oliver Perez's 2009.

The lesson, naturally, is that projecting pitchers is a tricky enterprise. With every stat on your side, that pitcher can still blow up on you. But using stats to produce likeliest outcomes is still key—especially key given the uncertainties of pitching.

I explained that to Ted, but he (and others) wanted to know about the Mets' winning streak, pointing out that the Mets "had recently shown a trend toward replacing veterans with cost-controlled young players with upside," referencing the replacement of Gary Matthews Jr. and Mike Jacobs on the roster.

As I explained in response, "I'm thrilled that the Mets have won eight of nine, and my hope is that they win their next eight of nine. But they've had successful streaks in the past. This is about making sure the Mets are successful for the long term, in 2015, and in many years after that."

I knew that for all my rhetoric, I needed to show Mets fans

some additional specifics to define myself. While Omar Minaya was still busy fixing the Mets, I hoped, there was a former GM of the Mets who represented, despite his successes, everything I didn't want to do once I was elected. His name was Steve Phillips, and it was time to challenge him to a debate.

Chapter 4

THE SEASON OF LIGHT,
THE SEASON OF DARKNESS

I T WAS THE best of times, it was the blurst of times." So
wrote a monkey employed by Charles Montgomery Burns,
"Last Exit to Springfield," Season 4, Episode 17.

Without question, that monkey was talking about the Mets
under Steve Phillips.

Under Phillips, the team earned two postseason berths, but
while he inherited an 88–74 team in 1997, he left the Mets a
66–95 mess in 2003. Under Phillips, they traded for Mike
Piazza; they traded for Mo Vaughn. They traded for Al Leiter;
they signed Kevin Appier to a five-year, $50 million contract.
They acquired Mike Hampton for the 2000 season; they tried
to sign Hampton to a seven-year, $105 million contract after the
2000 season.

And, unforgivably, they failed to sign Alex Rodriguez, the
crown jewel in the trove of free-agent mistakes by the franchise.
And every one of these mistakes did more than just negatively
affect the Mets' competitive advantage. As a fan, I felt them. I
got angry again just writing this chapter.

Like so many Americans, I still have stored-up frustration over lost Rule V draft picks.

Ultimately, the real problem with Phillips is that he ran the Mets in much the same way the housing bubble ran its course in the United States. Instead of building the foundation, he continued adding pieces to the top. Ultimately—surprise!—it all collapsed. Only errors by other general managers—a failure to take Phillips up on some lopsided trade proposals—prevented Phillips from leaving the organization as bereft of talent as it had been at any point in its history.

Living through it as a fan was alternately exhilarating and debilitating. After eleven years without any playoff appearances, the Mets of 1999 and 2000 were exciting, presented a diverse array of talent, and very nearly won a third World Series. But they were built on a house of cards built by mannequins. And the mannequins turned into pumpkins made of sand.

Also, most of the best players in the run were acquired by Joe McIlvaine, Phillips's predecessor.

Let's break down exactly where Phillips went wrong.

He took over in July of 1997, yet the weaknesses that led the 2000 team to fall short were created by Phillips in just a few months. In a ten-day span, from December 12 to December 22, 1997, he traded outfielders Alex Ochoa and Carl Everett, receiving outfielder Rich Becker from the Twins for Ochoa and reliever John Hudek from Houston for Everett.

The moves made little sense, even at the time. Ochoa's defensive skills—particularly a plus arm—made him a better fit as a fourth outfielder than Becker. Ochoa was two months younger than Becker and hit about the same against left-handed and right-handed pitchers, making him a steady option for all situations. Becker, on the other hand, was significantly worse against lefties, although to be fair he was bad against all kinds of pitching—he hit .190 for the Mets. It was a challenge trade, but none of the data points were on Phillips's side.

The Everett deal was even worse. Everett's play in the latter half of 1995 had given fans hope that the dark ages of 1991 to 1994 had finally ended. He'd struggled some in 1996 and 1997 with injuries, but remained an outfielder who could handle all three positions, displayed plus power and speed, and was just turning twenty-seven.

I'll be honest—none of us thought he was going to become a star (although he eventually did). But why trade him at that moment for Hudek, a thirty-one-year-old reliever coming off a 5.98 ERA season? Hudek was not a total washout, but he was never more than the fourth arm in any bullpen, before this trade or after—a spare part. Congratulations, Mets: You just gave up all the upside in a trade in exchange for a commodity freely available on the free-agent market, at any time of year.

Fast-forward to 2000. The Met outfield included Benny Agbayani, with an OPS+ of 122 (league average is 100, above 100 being better); Derek Bell, with an OPS+ of 98; and Jay Payton, with an OPS+ of 98. (Payton and Agbayani, incidentally, were acquired by the Mets before Phillips took over.)

Meanwhile, Alex Ochoa posted a 137 OPS+ with terrific defense for the Cincinnati Reds. Carl Everett's OPS+ was 135, with 34 home runs, for the Boston Red Sox.

In ten days in 1997, Phillips robbed the 2000 Mets of a truly dominant outfield.

This kind of inattention to detail continued to hobble the Mets even as Phillips thrilled fans with the Mike Piazza trade. His first draft produced Ty Wigginton and little else. The team was starved for back-end starting pitching, but Phillips allowed

Cory Lidle to go unprotected in the 1997 expansion draft and threw in Nelson Figueroa in a 1998 deal to acquire a hard-to-remember player named Willie Blair.

Even the successes of that time have a bucket-list quality to them, never a good sign when trying to foster long-term growth in a franchise. The unfortunate reality of baseball is that, from the moment a player has his breakout major-league season, he is like a new car driven off the lot: His owner can get less and less return as time goes on. During each of the six seasons when he is not yet eligible for free agency, his price tag goes up and he is under team control for less time.

By the time a player hits his early thirties, chances are he's a free agent, his peak years are behind him, and his cost is prohibitively expensive. So unless that player is uniquely talented or fills a need the team can't fill in any other way, signing players to long-term free-agent contracts at that point in their careers, or trading for them, is a sucker's bet. It's not that it never pays off—sometimes you get lucky. But let's face it, this kind of deal is a hallmark of bad management in any field: spending money on glitz rather than production, lacking faith in your own organizational talent, and consistently valuing the short term over the long.

Phillips did it again and again.

Robin Ventura was beloved by Mets fans, and with good reason: His performance in 1999 represented one of the finest seasons by any Met third baseman, pretty much ever. Phillips had signed him to a four-year, $31.5 million contract during the previous off-season. He turned thirty-one during that great year of '99, after four years of steadily declining production from '95 to '98, with OPS+ numbers of 132, 127, 112, and 105. Phillips got that great season from him in year one of the contract, but then

Ventura resumed his decline, putting up an OPS+ of 98 and 104 in his next two years. After the 2001 season, the Mets traded him to the Yankees for David Justice, who was in turn dealt to Oakland for the aging reliever Mark Guthrie and the forgettable Tyler Yates. The Mets managed to foot most of Justice's salary in the process.

Yates spent that year, like much of his career, in the minors. Guthrie had a respectable 2002 as the team's seventh-inning reliever (who cost the Mets about $8 million in total). Justice, by the way, had an OPS+ of 111 that year, better than anyone in the Mets outfield. The A's, who had him essentially for free, won 103 games.

The Ventura contract didn't pan out, but just when Phillips was about to get himself a decent return in that final year, he gave it away to a better team with a better GM.

Oh, but if the Ventura deal had been an isolated incident, it could've been forgiven. Sadly, it was not so. A few weeks before signing Ventura, Phillips signed the left-handed reliever Dennis Cook to a three-year, $6.6 million contract. Cook had been excellent for the Mets in 1998, with a 2.38 ERA. But he was also turning thirty-six. Signing a reliever, of any age, to a three-year contract is viewed by most GMs as asking for trouble; you can imagine how much sense it makes to sign a thirty-six-year-old to that kind of deal.

Cook had a 4.56 ERA over the next three seasons, including half a year with the Philadelphia Phillies. Phillips traded him for little return—he was just trying to recoup a few of the lost salary dollars.

Within a month of signing Cook, the Mets lost Scott Sauerbeck to the Pittsburgh Pirates in the Rule V draft. Sauerbeck made $901,667 total over three seasons. A decade younger than

Cook, his age twenty-seven to twenty-nine seasons were predictably far better than Cook's thirty-six to thirty-eight years. He pitched to a 3.56 ERA over four-plus seasons with Pittsburgh. He could have done the same thing with the Mets, saving the team another $6 million or so in the process. The amount of effort it would've taken was essentially nil—protect Sauerbeck in the Rule V draft, and don't sign Cook.

Look—I know these sound like small criticisms. A reliever here, an overpaid player there—are they really such mortal sins? In a word, yes. Think back to the World Series, all the things you hear about unsung heroes and bit players in the post-season drama. Who are these guys, if not little deals that went right? Every team with money can go sign a famous free agent like Pedro Martinez or Carlos Beltran (unless that free agent is A-Rod). And every team knows to hang on to great young players like Wright and Reyes (as long as they fail to trade them). But the whole picture of how a team is managed, who the role players are, what the clubhouse mix is like—that's what GMs have to do week in and week out. And that's what Steve Phillips wouldn't, or couldn't, accomplish.

It wasn't hard, for a fan like me at least, to see that Phillips didn't think there were any answers to be had in players under thirty. He traded minor-league slugger Roberto Petagine, who went on to a fantastic career in Japan. Therefore, when John Olerud left as a free agent, Phillips's answer was the well-traveled Todd Zeile, who gave the Mets a mediocre 102 OPS+ over two seasons for more than $11 million, plus another $4 million for the Rockies to take him in the final year of his contract. (The team wanted to clear some of its salary commitments to make way for thirty-four-year-old Mo Vaughn.)

Phillips also traded for thirty-three-year-old Lenny Harris, thirty-three-year-old Wayne Kirby, thirty-one-year-old Greg McMichael, thirty-nine-year-old Tony Phillips, thirty-two-year-old Willie Blair, and thirty-five-year-old Bobby Bonilla, and signed a forty-year-old Rickey Henderson and thirty-year-old Craig Paquette. And that's not the complete list—that's just the thirtysomethings he brought in between July and December 1998.

Did I mention the Mets are still paying Bobby Bonilla today, in 2011, twelve years after the last game he played for them? Let's save this for another time.

Let's go back to cars for a minute. This strategy is like buying a ten-year-old car and hoping to get factory-showroom performance. It just doesn't make sense. If someone did this with cars, he'd be ridiculed—or at least very poor. But Phillips, and many other lesser GMs, think of this as acquiring players with a track record. A track record is what already happened.

There's a fan aspect to this, too. Consider Benny Agbayani, one of the few players from the farm whom Phillips let contribute to his teams—after his veteran alternatives washed out, of course.

Agbayani got the call in May 1999 and promptly caught fire. He homered in his first game. He tripled in his second game. He had his first multihomer game in his eighth contest. By the end of May, he was hitting .442, slugging .905, and had 10 extra-base hits in 52 at bats.

I had first seen Agbayani play as an awkward twenty-one-year-old for Pittsfield of the New York–Penn League. He'd hit just 2 home runs that season, batting .251, and showed no signs of becoming a useful major-league player.

So we were listening to the eighth game Agbayani ever played in as a family on May 20, 1999, as we all drove home from Bard

College, making the three-hour trip home after my sophomore year of college. My father asked me about Agbayani and I reminded him that we'd seen him in Pittsfield, and we began to count all the Mets we'd seen there who'd made it to the major leagues, taking that epic trip through the system after starting at the lowest of low minors.

I also told him Agbayani was a "Triple-A hitter."

I pretty much never lived that down. Imagine, if you will, listening to or watching Mets games every night, with the Triple-A hitter smashing extra-base hits in droves. Another home run, another needling from my father.

But the lesson of Benny Agbayani is twofold. For one thing, Mets fans loved him. Adored him. Long before he hit the game-winning home run off Aaron Fultz in Game 3 of the 2000 NLDS, Agbayani was absolutely beloved by the fans. He'd come through the minors. He looked awkward as hell in left field. But the man had power. He was our awkward left fielder.

The other, vital lesson is that there simply aren't Triple-A hitters. Not many of them, anyway. The guys who earn that title generally do so on the strength of many Triple-A at-bats and a handful of major-league at-bats. Show me a large number of hitters who succeed over the long term at Triple-A but fail in 1,000, 1,500, 2,000 major-league at-bats, and maybe I'll reconsider.

Instead what we have, along with those small sample failures, are a large number of hitters who succeeded at Triple-A, failed at first in the major leagues, then succeeded, usually pretty wildly. A player like Agbayani, who in Triple-A had posted an .841 OPS in 1997 and .859 in 1998 before exploding in 1999, was a damn good bet to post .800+ OPS seasons with the Mets, as he did in 1999 and 2000.

There are no Triple-A hitters. Alas, Steve Phillips seemed to believe the exact opposite.

And there's a lesson here about who the fans will lionize, too. A popular myth is that New York fans will neither tolerate rebuilding nor attach themselves to anyone less than the best. For all his success, Benny Agbayani wasn't the best—not even close. But Mets fans loved his foibles, his awkward pursuit of fly balls in left field, and adored his long home runs. Sure, there's a team in town that demands the best in everything. But if Mets fans wanted that, they'd have shifted from Queens to the Bronx a long time ago. Mets fans have remarkable patience for their large-market team to build from within; they want to see someone take his lumps as he travels up the organizational ladder, then bloom into an everyday player. I still miss watching Benny Agbayani.

Didn't matter, though: Phillips's drafts continued to be busts. Geoff Goetz, Jason Tyner, Billy Traber, and Bobby Keppel were the first-round picks from 1997 to 2000; none of them ever played in a meaningful game for the Mets. Meanwhile he was still getting old, mediocre players by trade. The 1999 trade deadline brought in thirty-one-year-old Mandy Romero, thirty-eight-year-old Billy Taylor, thirty-four-year-old Darryl Hamilton, thirty-one-year-old Chuck McElroy, and thirty-six-year-old Shawon Dunston. Some of them helped, some of them didn't. All of them were patchwork solutions with only downside to what remained of their careers.

And so it continued into 2000. Traber, who pitched in one Triple-A game before being dealt to the Indians, was the best of that year's draft. When shortstop Rey Ordonez got injured, Phillips decided the answer was Mike Bordick, a thirty-four-year-old with declining range and a career OPS+

of 83. He traded four prospects for him—*four!*—including Melvin Mora, who went on to hit 148 home runs for Baltimore from 2001 to 2008. Bordick, meanwhile, posted an OPS+ of 76 as a Met and was let go after one season. He made $3 million in 2000, incidentally.

But it's all prelude to perhaps the most massive screw-up in the team's history, bigger than trading Nolan Ryan, bigger than trading Tom Seaver, bigger than anything.

The New York Mets failed to sign Alex Rodriguez.

Look—I know what you think happened. The Rangers gave him the biggest contract in baseball history, then got tired of him. In 2003, the Red Sox made an aggressive move for him but couldn't get it approved by the league. The Yankees stepped in, paid the big bucks, and the two most unpopular, successful forces in all of baseball were inevitably united. But that's not the whole story. And before you tell me that you never liked him, just hear me out.

Not signing Rodriguez was a disaster.

Let's begin with the basics. Following the 2000 season, Alex Rodriguez hit the free-agent market. As most of us know, he had outrageous success at an obscenely early age, batting .358/.414/.631 at age twenty and playing tremendous defense at shortstop. And because he hadn't been to college and barely played in the minors, he'd reached six years of MLB service time earlier than most.

This is the trade-off one makes between signing long-term contracts for rookies and for veteran stars: While younger players have more peak years left, older players have a more established record of success. Few twenty-four-year-olds have more than one or two great years under their belts, while most thirty-one-year-olds have played through their primes.

Alex Rodriguez, in the winter of 2000, was twenty-four years old, and over his previous five seasons had hit 184 home runs, posted an OPS+ of 143, and gave Seattle one of the best defenders in the league at shortstop, arguably the most important defensive position. It is essentially impossible to conceive of a more valuable free agent hitting the market in baseball history. He had the track record, the talent, and the ambition. And there was no uncertainty about it: We knew. We knew he was a superstar on par with the greatest in baseball history. We knew that his best years were still to come. Oh, and we knew one other thing.

Alex Rodriguez wanted, above all else, to play for the New York Mets.

Rodriguez was born in New York. He came of age as the great Met teams of the 1980s reigned supreme. He wanted the big stage, and although he might've had more of that with the Yankees, they had a bit of an obstacle at shortstop: Derek Jeter. And A-Rod didn't want to share the spotlight. It was a perfect fit. And even better for the Mets, it was one of the few times they wouldn't need to outbid the Yankees to bring a truly great player to Queens.

Not only did the Mets fail to sign him, not only did they fail to even make an offer on the best free agent there ever was (and likely ever will be, for reasons we will discuss later), but Steve Phillips did something really extraordinary: He went out and publicly criticized Rodriguez, calling him "a twenty-four-and-one player." (In case it isn't clear—that's Phillips-speak for "selfish.")

In other words, he slammed the door on Rodriguez ever coming to the Mets, then and for as long as he was in charge.

But wait, you might be saying. How do we know the Mets

could've pulled this off? Maybe the Wilpons simply didn't have the money for this kind of thing.

In a way, you might be right—but whose fault is that? In 1998 and '99, you could've found enough to cover two years of A-Rod's salary just by not overpaying for the Dennis Cooks and Robin Venturas of the world. And not only that, just after Rodriguez signed with the Rangers, Phillips went out and spent big money to get . . . Kevin Appier and Mo Vaughn.

The Mets signed Appier to a four-year, $42 million deal in the 2000 off-season. Then, after Appier's first season, they dealt him to Anaheim for Mo Vaughn, who was owed another $46.6 million. I'll save you some math—this comes to about $55 million over four seasons. During the same period, A-Rod made about $100 million. Is it the same amount of money? No. But then again, Appier won only 11 games for the Mets, and Vaughn had the worst three years of his career—most of them on the disabled list.

You get what you overpay for.

By the way, you can be sure that extra $45 million could've been saved somewhere else. How about $18 million for Roger Cedeno, whose four-year contract became an albatross almost immediately, and $9 million for David Weathers, a middle reliever? Anyway—you get the picture.

But it could have been even simpler. Once Rodriguez turned down a pair of long-term contract offers from Seattle in 1998, that he would hit the free-agent market after the 2000 season was known to everybody. This was LeBron ten years before LeBron, except baseball has no salary cap or max salary offer. Only the rich teams were going to be in the bidding. And the Mets were one of them.

Steve Phillips should have gone to the Wilpons in 1998 and

said, "Look, I don't know if it will cost $20 million, $25 million per season, but there's every reason in the world to sign Alex Rodriguez if we have the chance. How do we plan, financially, to make that possible?"

And then maybe the Wilpons would have said, Okay, but don't spend $6 million on Dennis Cook. Don't throw $31.5 million at one productive season by Robin Ventura. Or $15 million for two seasons of Todd Zeile.

Sigh.

Did I mention who was the shortstop the Mets employed instead of Alex Rodriguez? That would be Rey Ordonez.

The Mets wasted $19 million on him from 2000 to 2003. And what did they get for their money?

During the years from 2001 to 2003, while A-Rod was in Texas making three All-Star teams, winning three Gold Gloves and an MVP award, hitting 156 home runs and scoring 382 runs, the Mets had Rey Ordonez. During those three years, Ordonez hit 7 home runs.

Ordonez was a flashy defensive shortstop, but his conditioning had already begun to erode his defensive skills. And he was, and I can't stress this enough, the worst hitter in baseball. Worse than many pitchers. Absolutely, brutally awful, and with no visible signs of improvement from his ridiculously poor rookie year of 1996 until his final season with the Mets in 2002.

Let's be charitable for a moment. Ordonez was a defensive shortstop, and for a time one of the best in the league. Plus, his comparatively cheap salary cleared room for other guys on the roster, guys like Appier, Vaughn, Cedeno, and Weathers. This must be what Phillips meant about not wanting "twenty-four-and-one" players. He wanted guys he could afford, who helped the *team* come together, and who excelled at intangibles like clubhouse leadership and defense. He wanted champions.

The 2001 Mets went 82–80, finishing third in their division. In 2002 and 2003, they finished in last place.

Of Ordonez, Cedeno, Appier, and Vaughn, whose collective salaries could've been swapped for A-Rod, only Cedeno was still on the roster by the end of the '03 season. He batted .267 with no power, little speed, and played the outfield, in Keith Hernandez's words, "like he was being chased by a bee." Consider that both Ordonez and Rodriguez were regulars from 1996 to 2002. During that time, among players with at least 3,000 plate appearances, Rodriguez's OPS+ mark of 148 was thirteenth in all of baseball, and he had 293 home runs. But remember, that's thirteenth-best at any position, and Rodriguez was also playing superb defense at shortstop. The next-closest shortstop was Nomar Garciaparra, at 136.

And if you scroll all the way down to the bottom of the list, the very last name on the list, you'll find . . . Rey Ordonez.

Rey Ordonez had an OPS+ of 57. He hit 8 home runs, or around one per season. (It usually came in September.) He trails hitters like Neifi Perez, Rey Sanchez, and Deivi Cruz. They were all defense-first middle infielders known for their light bats. And they absolutely dominated Rey Ordonez as hitters.

Here's my favorite fact about this list: The next twelve from the bottom, in terms of OPS+, all played for multiple teams, usually three or four. In other words, offensive production that putrid means you find another team. Your team doesn't want you anymore.

The next-lowest OPS+ over that time to stay with one team? Dan Wilson, a catcher with Seattle. His OPS+ was 86, which is actually around average for a catcher. No one close to

Rey Ordonez kept on playing regularly. No one came close to Ordonez offensively, period.

For an extra $20 million per season—again, assuming it even took matching Texas's offer for the Mets to get A-Rod (he's told me he would have taken less to play in New York)—the Mets could have upgraded from the worst offensive player of his time to one of the absolute best, entering his prime, without sacrificing defense at the key defensive position on the diamond.

You may say that it wouldn't have mattered, given Steve Phillips's propensity for acquiring over-thirty mediocrities. I can't really argue with you. No amount of A-Rod greatness in 2002 or 2003 would have made a winner out of teams built on Jeromy Burnitz, Roberto Alomar, and Pedro Astacio.

Besides, you are saying, Steve Phillips excelled at both drafting poorly and trading the young talent he did have. I can't really argue with that, either. You can assemble a virtual All-Star lineup of players Phillips traded, or attempted to trade, as Met minor leaguers. Roberto Petagine at first, Melvin Mora at second, Jose Reyes at shortstop (tried to deal him for Roberto Alomar), David Wright at third (tried to trade him for Jose Cruz Jr.), an outfield of Nelson Cruz, Jason Bay, and Endy Chavez in center (long before he excelled for the Mets, Phillips lost him in the Rule V draft). All they'd need is a catcher.

By the way, the total haul for Phillips in exchange for those players? A washed-up Alomar, Cruz Jr., Yuri Sanchez, Mike Bordick, Steve Reed, Jason Middlebrook, Jorge Velandia, and $50,000 (the fee for a Rule V draft pick).

So it isn't as if the failure to sign Rodriguez represents the single move that made or broke Steve Phillips's tenure with the Mets. But this mishap is simply the centerpiece of a six-year reign that began with the Mets at 88 wins and on the rise, and ended six years later with the Mets at 66–95 and in utter disrepair. And imagine, just imagine, if he'd succeeded in dealing Wright and Reyes as well, leaving the Mets without the talent primarily responsible for the success they had under Omar Minaya.

A debate with Steve Phillips would have been more than just a useful means of showing the fans what I wouldn't do as general manager. It would have been cathartic. And based on his recent writings, it seemed as if Phillips wanted to have precisely that debate.

Chapter 5

A DAY (THAT WILL LIVE
IN INFAMY?)

S TEVE PHILLIPS'S POST-METS career has been rocky, to say the least. Following his dismissal, he landed a nice gig from 2005 to 2009 with ESPN, but they used him in a lot of odd bits of television, like pretend press conferences as general manager of teams he didn't run. He would often, inexplicably, debate himself in a segment called "Phillips vs. Phillips." And then, in 2009, he was fired for allegedly having an affair with a production assistant—something he'd had extra incentive to avoid after his sexual-harassment case from his time with the Mets in 1998.

In 2010 he did occasional spots on WFAN and wrote a column for the online publication AOL Fanhouse. And the one he penned on May 17, as I actively planned my run, seemed targeted at me directly. Entitled "Think You Can Be GM? You Have No Idea," Phillips wrote:

> As a former general manager, I often get approached by fans who vent about their teams and general managers. They don't like the players the GM acquired or they are frustrated

by the inactivity of the man in charge. Fans love their team and they believe they know what is best for their club. They believe any idiot could be a GM. I have heard comments like "I mean come on, how hard can it be? I won my fantasy league last year and I did it by making a few great trades." . . . What I have come to understand is that *everybody believes they can be a general manager.* That makes me realize that NOBODY UNDERSTANDS WHAT THE GENERAL MANAGER'S JOB REALLY ENTAILS!

The capital letters, by the way, were his. Phillips went on to provide revelations throughout the column, including that GMs oversee not only the major-league roster, but the minors as well! The GM oversees the draft! The GM needs to be in contact with team owners! The GM needs to give interviews! The GM needs to speak with team trainers, to know if players are hurt! The GM needs to speak to other GMs about potential trades!

And . . . that's it. Now, maybe he's right—maybe most people *don't* think about minor-league players or realize that the medical reports on injured players need to be evaluated. But not me. There are days when it seems like all I do is think about minor-league players. And don't even get me started on the Mets training staff.

Better still, Phillips appeared to be taking credit for . . . a minor-league system that produced the horrific trades mentioned in the last chapter, drafts that produced a handful of useful major-league players, and the trades that crippled the roster for half a decade.

But clearly, Phillips felt strongly about this idea that some electric-fence-type line separated him, and other people who had been general managers, from, well, me. And I thought it would be useful to give him the opportunity to present that case. Through a contact, I got Phillips's e-mail address and wrote him the following e-mail:

Dear Steve,

. My name is Howard Megdal. As you have probably heard, I am running for general manager of the New York Mets. (For more details, visit MegdalforGM.com.) As someone who has followed your career with great interest, I have noticed that in recent weeks you have taken great pains to explain what you, a former general manager, would do in terms of running a baseball team. For instance, on Monday you wrote a piece entitled, "Here's How a GM Sizes Up Trade Market."

But even clearer is how sure you are that while many people (for example, me) want to be general manager of a baseball team, you also wrote (caps yours), "NOBODY UNDERSTANDS WHAT THE GENERAL MANAGER'S JOB REALLY ENTAILS!"

In order to better understand any gap that exists between my plans once I am elected and your experience as actual GM of the New York Mets, I propose that we have a friendly debate over my candidacy for general manager, your experience as general manager, and the future direction of the New York Mets. Matthew Artus of NJ.com has graciously agreed to moderate, and we would be open to a debate either online or in person.

Please let me know if this would be amenable to you. As an aspiring GM, I think this would be immensely valuable, and could go a long way toward reminding fans (and potential front offices) of your decisions while running the New York Mets. I look forward to hearing from you.

Sincerely,
Howard Megdal

While I waited for a response, some fascinating dynamics began to play themselves out around my candidacy and the extent to which the Mets were listening. Before I made my announcement, I reached out to a high-level executive in the New York Mets organization. I had no intention of trying to catch the Wilpons by surprise—indeed, these were the men I wanted to hire me, or at the very least, to listen to what I had to say.

The man I spoke to was, and is, a powerful voice within the organization. Out of the many contacts I'd made with the Mets and throughout baseball, I knew he alone would be the most likely to provide a conduit. In the interest of protecting his identity, he will be known only as Deep Swoboda in these pages. But Mets fans should consider themselves extremely fortunate that he was hired by the organization. Also, Deep Swoboda is not his real name.

Deep Swoboda and I spoke by phone a few days before my announcement, and I sent him detailed information about my campaign. I wanted him, the Wilpons, and the organization to understand the difference between trying to bring down Omar Minaya and what I was doing. And I wanted to know that the Wilpons wouldn't view my candidacy with anger—that would defeat the very purpose of running. Deep Swoboda made it clear that the Mets wouldn't be able to endorse my candidacy—the team, after all, already had a GM. But he could find out if they'd stand in my way.

Look, if Omar Minaya had begun to operate the Mets with LOGIC, TRANSPARENCY, and PASSION, I'd have happily endorsed him to continue as general manager. Truth be told, I wasn't in this for the glory, not really. I just wanted the Mets to win! I'd spoken with Minaya several times, and each time I'd come away thinking he was a nice man who was in over his head. Our first encounter was a one-on-one at Shea Stadium prior to the 2007 Subway Series opener against the Yankees. This was Minaya at the height of his reputation, with the Mets appearing ready to take over the city, and Oliver Perez, having looked sharp all season, about to pitch eight innings against the Yankees to bring his ERA down to 2.90.

In my conversation with Minaya, I'd hoped for a nugget about what convinced the wily GM to get Pittsburgh to include Perez in the trade he'd completed the year before. Was it the word of some scout? Had he noticed a problem in Perez's delivery to be fixed?

Minaya stayed reliably vague. It may have been simple strategy; I was media, after all. But this was old news unlikely to turn into headlines. And it was hard to come away from the conversation convinced he knew much about Perez, even after he'd been Mets property for nearly a year.

I'll be honest. I didn't think, before or during my campaign, that Minaya was a great GM. But he had some things going for him. He was good at marketing, he was likeable, he handled the press well—as long as the team was winning. If Minaya, even at this late date, had delegated to the right advisers, I felt that things could have changed for the Mets overnight. LOGIC, TRANSPARENCY, and PASSION were not just the pillars of my campaign but qualities I genuinely believed would turn the team into a winner. And though Minaya had not (in my opinion, at least) displayed these qualities, particularly the first two, during his run as general manager, I wanted both him and the Wilpons to know what I believed it would take for the team to turn its fortunes around.

So Deep Swoboda sent my speech to the powers that ran the New York Mets. At the very least, I knew they had my plan. Would they be bitterly opposed to an outsider presenting an alternate view of what the team could be? Or had the Wilpons simply never been presented with this alternative, a basic view of how a baseball team must be run to maximize success?

That was my guess. It certainly wasn't in their best interest to spend big money but miss the playoffs, to have one public-relations disaster after another. Simply put, I didn't believe they'd found a GM who had brought this basic vision to the table, not since Frank Cashen left in 1991. Maybe they'd pick me—I hoped they would. But I also knew that, as far as they were concerned, I was just another reporter, or maybe even just another fan. And if that meant they were going to ignore me, well, then at least I wanted those ideas out there. Let the Wilpons hear what I had to say, and then, if they still chose chaos, well, I'd done what I could do for the Mets, for my sanity, for the future games I'd attend with my family. My conscience would be clear.

So as I waited to hear back from Steve Phillips, I got the following note from Deep Swoboda in response to my e-mail with details about my candidacy, including my introductory speech.

Thanks Howard. Saw the pick up on your announcement. Congrats. All the best.

Maybe that doesn't sound like much to you. Maybe it sounds like a friendly e-mail from someone who isn't in a position to really help me. Maybe it's just north of an automated-reply e-mail. But that's not what I saw. *Saw the pick up on your announcement.* That meant a person in the Mets organization—a high-ranking member—had sat at his computer and read news articles about my candidacy. In other words: The Mets were listening. The door was open to seeing the Mets run in a fundamentally different way. And maybe, just maybe, I'd be the one to walk through that door. *All the best*, he'd said. The best!

In the meantime, I had to convince the public to support me. After all, these were now the stakes: If the positive vision of LOGIC, TRANSPARENCY, and PASSION didn't motivate the fan base, then what good was I? I was supposed to be representing a movement, and I believed I was. But what if no one cared? What if I was shouting into a void? The Wilpons would quickly conclude that only winning would earn the support of the fans, and they would simply return to their business.

I believed otherwise. I believed that if fans saw an intelligent effort to run the organization well, and a management team that clearly cared as much as they did, the end result didn't need to be a World Series every year. Mets fans would be excited to be a part of something, to have hope and excitement every year and young, talented players to pull for. We wanted energy, enthusiasm, not just manufactured trophies. Only Yankees fans expect that.

So I did what candidates do: I engaged the voters. Everywhere I went, if I saw someone in a Mets hat, wearing a Mets shirt, I'd explain my mission. What I found, before I even had the chance to mention my campaign, was that people were upset.

Seriously upset. Like, couldn't start talking about the Mets without getting angry, red-faced, extremely critical. We'd be in public places and it wouldn't matter. People were really mad at the New York Mets. And these were the people in the orange-and-blue hats and shirts.

I decided it was time to get out the vote and had an idea how to do it: primaries. Just like a political candidate, I was looking for a mandate from the masses. Having seen that people were angry, I felt that we just needed to be heard. So I called a few friends who have Mets blogs and asked them to host a primary for me. No, there were no other candidates to run *against*, exactly—unless you counted Minaya. But we would have a vote, and if the people wanted me to be GM, well, they'd say so.

Every single blogger I spoke to about a primary immediately supported the idea. Think about that for a second. People who are so interested in the New York Mets that they began a forum, on their own time, to write about the team were universally convinced that the management of the team was better left to me, on the basis of a single phone call, than the people in charge at the time.

That's about more than just wins and losses. That's a group of people who didn't feel spoken to, either directly or through the way the team operated. I knew I could do more.

But where to start? There were so many people to reach out to, so many preparations to make. I traveled to Citi Field in June for a game against the Padres with my cousin and videographer, Lauren Krueger, intent upon getting video for my first campaign commercial. I figured at Citi Field, where fans were still congregating—still *paying* to be a part of this Mets experience—perhaps the mood would be different.

It wasn't. People embraced my vision for the Mets about as

quickly as they shook my orange-foam-fingered hand. I didn't promise people their favorite manager would return, or a World Series every year—just a basic logic underlying player moves, a complete explanation of what principles caused me to make those moves, and the guarantee that no one would care about the process more than I would.

One of my brain trust, Dan Szymborski, was hosting my online "listening tour" at Baseball Think Factory. The site was where I met Dan, the editor in chief. Back in college I'd met a lot of people thinking intelligently about baseball there. Many of them were now my peers in the media: Dan, for instance, now split his time between BTF and ESPN.com.

Online, the conversation tended to range from haranguing to attempts at humor, but the discussions were different in person. When we finished shooting for the first commercial, I walked to my seats in the Promenade, Section 508. It was a Thursday afternoon so there weren't many people in my section—a sad preview of how things would look at the end of the season.

A couple sitting behind us asked what we'd been filming for, and I told them all about the campaign. They'd been Mets fans since 1964, had attended Shea Stadium that very first year it opened.

"This is our last game this year," the husband said sadly. "There's not much reason to keep coming back."

And that was the hardest thing of all—not the angry fans, but the ones who had given up. Every empty seat in that stadium on a Thursday afternoon represented someone who had once been like me but whom the Mets had lost. And when you lose baseball from your life, it isn't as if it gets replaced with something better. Instead, for 162 games a year, three hours at a time, a person gets to do something not as fulfilling, not as emotionally engaging, not as intellectually rewarding. This is loss on a massive, 1962 Mets level.

So as hard as it was, I knew that, despite late-night feedings for my two-month-old and a full slate of writing each week, I needed to find the time to continue talking to people, reaching out, seeing if I could convince Mets fans, one by one, that a better way forward existed for our favorite baseball team.

I was mindful, though, there were the fires of the present to put out. As Steve Phillips had so vociferously reminded me, the job of the GM is big and time-consuming. In June, that meant a discussion of catcher Rod Barajas and a contract extension.

One of the reasons the Mets had been on an upswing was the performance of Barajas, a thirty-four-year-old catcher the Mets had signed after failing to get Bengie Molina. (I wouldn't have pursued Molina myself, but that's probably not worth getting into.) Barajas, the fallback option, had blasted 11 home runs in April and May, making him the unlikely team leader in the category.

The chances were slim that Barajas had reached a new talent level at this point in his career—we knew this power surge wouldn't last. The engaging backstop was a favorite of the writers, myself included, but I knew that gravity was bound to take its toll on his stats. The fall would likely be precipitous.

So when I read a column by *Newsday*'s David Lennon on June 12, 2010, entitled "Mets Would Be Wise to Re-Sign Barajas," I was surprised. The Mets had signed Barajas to a one-year, $1 million contract. Even if he kept up this pace, they'd have the chance to re-sign him at the end of the season. And not only was the pace likely to slacken, he'd only played in 120 or more games twice in his career. Did the market for thirty-five-year-old catchers really promise to be so rich that the Mets needed to get in early?

Even as I aspired to greater things, I knew my work as a reporter was never done. If I were in the front office, I would simply have ignored a column like this, knowing it was nothing more than temporary excitement. But someone else was making the decisions, and I was worried. I wanted the world to know about Josh Thole, the minor-league catcher who was absolutely on fire at Triple-A. He needed a shot, and Barajas would be nothing more than an expensive roadblock.

This was Dennis Cook and Scott Sauerbeck all over again. This would be the Mets wasting money on reduced performance with no future upside. It would stunt the development of Thole, who could give them league-average hitting at catcher for league-minimum salary, and leave a gaping hole in the future at the position when Barajas naturally cratered.

And it was further proof to me that I could separate between a fan's view and what I wanted for my team. As a fan, it was a pleasure to see a nice man like Rod Barajas in a Mets uniform. I enjoyed cheering for him. As a writer, he made my life much easier—I knew I would get the chance to hear his interpretation of what took place during the game, and my story would be richer for including his quotes.

But I also knew, logically, that he was the wrong fit for a contract extension.

What was infuriating is that the people running baseball operations for the Mets didn't seem to get it, either. And that was so strange to me. Here I was, blessed with arguably less of a stake in the operations of the New York Mets, and I understood it. I was far from the only one, too. No one else was stepping up to run the ballclub, but many other writers could see the folly in much of what the Mets did as it was happening.

And the more I thought about it, the more that made sense. No job we hold consumes us emotionally like a baseball team. No job we could ever have would offer the moment I experienced on June 17, with the Mets facing the Cleveland Indians on the road.

With the Mets batting in the top of the eighth, the alarm sounded—Mirabelle's cry came through the monitor. Instantly, Rachel and I swung into action. While she prepared to feed the baby, I changed her and brought her to the bedroom. Mirabelle's feed began in time to see Jose Reyes triple to put the Mets ahead, 6–4, and lasted through the top of the ninth.

Having fulfilled the necessary eating and burping, Mirabelle was as happy and alert as could be. I collected her into my lap and turned her to face the television. I'd read what the American Association of Pediatrics said—no television until age two. Most of the time, I listened—but there were moral considerations at play here. No human, especially a baby with a developing brain, should go without baseball until age two. The idea that it would hamper intellectual acuity was clearly propagated by someone who never watched a baseball game. It seemed downright un-American.

One of the simple pleasures my daughter gave me from the earliest months was an attention span far greater than I had any right to expect. She watched the game intently with me as I explained the individual situations. With the Mets trying to protect their lead in the bottom of the ninth, I told her about the importance of keeping a runner off base. In a 6–4 game, it would bring the tying run to the plate. She gripped my index finger tightly with her entire hand when Shin-Soo Choo singled, then stole second base. Was she caught up in the drama? It was hard to conclude anything else. Even Rachel, who had been skeptical about my insistence on playing Vin Scully broadcasts through an earbud I placed in her belly button during pregnancy, admitted that Mirabelle appeared to be fully absorbed in the game.

Carlos Santana, the dangerous rookie catcher, ran a count full against closer Francisco Rodriguez. I took Mirabelle carefully through the at-bat, explaining how the chances of success by the batter change so mightily depending on whether the count goes 1–2 or 2–1, the importance of throwing a strike with the count full to avoid bringing up the winning run, and raised both of her arms in the air when K-Rod got Santana to chase strike three. Was it me, or had she helped with this celebratory gesture, just a little? Two outs.

Rachel always got nervous with Rodriguez on the mound, a natural response for anyone who has lived through the era of Mariano Rivera and views other closers with suspicion by comparison. She'd put aside her reading material—*What to Expect the First Year*—and was fully absorbed in the game as well.

For Mirabelle's benefit, the count once again went full. Baseball had her attention for the first time and had no intention of disappointing. When Travis Hafner swung and missed at strike three, K-Rod pumped his fist and pointed to the sky, which is where Mirabelle could be found as I threw her into the air to celebrate. She smiled broadly, happy at all the attention, while Rachel cheered Mirabelle and a Mets victory simultaneously.

Had she also experienced what a hard-fought victory by her favorite baseball team felt like? I was desperate to know and equally certain that I'd never find out. The meaning of these early experiences would be forgotten by the time she had the gift of speech. I'd never know if my bedtime stories, usually taken from MLBTradeRumors.com, had any effect. What happens to the infant mind when the last thing she hears about at night is Cliff Lee's possible landing spot? Would science ever allow us to find out?

In that moment I realized, too, that I needed to communicate to Mets fans that there was a connection between rooting for a team that avoided long-term contracts to thirty-four-year-old catchers and the chance to toss your beaming daughter into the air because your favorite team just won.

So I refused to sugarcoat my thoughts to conform to the individual desires of each fan I spoke to on my listening tour. When someone tried to persuade me to simply replace Jerry Manuel as the manager with Bobby Valentine, I'd explain that I didn't believe managerial motivation could turn Jeff Francoeur into a useful hitter or Luis Castillo back into the player he was in his twenties or give Oliver Perez his fastball back. Hearing that Carlos Beltran or David Wright or Jose Reyes was the problem, I'd remind that fan of the tremendous success each player was having, and of the failings of those around the three stars in the star-crossed finishes of 2007 and 2008. I'd explain rationally what I wanted to do. And remarkably, I came away from those conversations with more support. Not always, of course. But many, many times.

Mets fans didn't want success all the time. They just wanted to hear what was really going on, and why.

But how could I explain that to Mets fans? That there was a connection between needlessly rushing along Jenrry Mejia, the twenty-year-old the Mets had already brought to the big leagues, and the success of the 2012, 2013, 2014 Mets?

Even more important, I knew I had to get people to engage.

At the moment, it seemed to me that they just wanted to complain. And this wasn't something rare. My literature adviser in college had once said that every writer needed to be at odds, in some way, with the world. But to convert that energy into pushing for positive change? This wouldn't be easy, and I knew that without fan support the movement would come to nothing.

With voting set to begin the following week, I recorded a script for my first ad, trying to balance all of these themes, hoping that Lauren would provide a coherent visual accompaniment. My good friend and composer Akie Bermiss recorded an original score to accentuate my message to fans.

I'm Howard Megdal, and I'm running to be the next general manager of the New York Mets. Writing about baseball is my job, but I have lived and loved the New York Mets since I was six years old. Together, we've celebrated when the Mets were magical, but too often lately we've felt the stinging taunts of other fans wound us in defeat. I'm running to become the next general manager because I believe there's a better way. Under my watch, the Mets will operate with LOGIC, TRANSPARENCY, and PASSION.

Go to MegdalforGM.com to learn more about how we can make sure the next generations' Mets are as amazing as they should be. In the coming months, you will have the chance to vote for me in twenty primaries on the Internet. With a mandate of millions of fans at my back, that job is sure to follow.

But this is about more than a job. Elect me and we will take control of the team that governs our emotions day after day. Let's give my baby daughter a lifetime of happy recaps. Let's take back the Mets. Ya gotta believe, but just believin' isn't enough anymore. I'm Howard Megdal, and I approved this message.

It was the best I could do. On June 21, the ad would drop. Then voting would begin. Those who thought I was crazy would have the chance to weigh in—and so would the people I reached.

That movement would take place without Steve Phillips, unfortunately. I'd received an e-mail from Phillips responding to my letter. Did he wish to inform people, in a more robust intellectual setting, about how I HAD NO IDEA how to be a general manager? Did he have words of wisdom for my pursuit of the job?

"No thank you. Good luck."

That was it. That was the whole e-mail. No "Sincerely, Steve." No "By the way, sorry about trading Jason Bay." Nothing else from Mr. Phillips, the man who debated himself on ESPN? (Seriously, I invite you to pause reading this book so you can go look it up on Youtube.)

But apparently my call to supporters to likewise petition Phillips had generated a significant response. Later that same day, I received the following letter:

Hey Howard.

Your email asking to debate Steve Phillips, and the emails of a number of your readers making the same request, have come into our site's tipline. (We do not make Steve's email address available to the public, for obvious reasons, so the emails end up coming to our tipline.) I wanted to let you know that we got the requests and that Steve has been made aware of them. However, Steve has informed me, as well as you, I believe, that he is not interested in your offer.

If you have any further questions, you can email me.

Thanks
Andrew Johnson, MLB Editor, AOL FanHouse

Well, okay, it was just a longer way of saying no thanks. But I also felt something—recognition. Andrew Johnson—and the three (three!) other people he'd copied on the e-mail—saw my request as legitimate. I wasn't just shouting into a void anymore. I had motivated someone to *do* something, even though that thing was to tell me no. It provided me with the same lift I imagined presidential candidates feel when they win the Iowa straw poll. Sure, it didn't mean anything in terms of an actual vote count or delegates. But I had moved people, at least, to discuss it. To tell Steve Phillips they wanted to hear my ideas. To discuss LOGIC, TRANSPARENCY, and PASSION. Interested observers wanted to hear the difference between the way Steve Phillips had run the Mets—not dramatically different from the way they'd been run for twenty years—and the changes I would bring.

I had begun to bridge the gap between the crazy person who writes letters—what are columns of baseball analysis, after all, but those letters, mass-distributed?—and an executive putting a coherent plan of action into effect to transform my favorite baseball team.

The sanest part about what I wanted to bring to the Mets was that we already knew it would work. Indeed, so many of the principles Billy Beane used to make Oakland a winner were derided by fans in large markets. Wouldn't work in a big town, according to plenty of critics.

But I knew precisely what it would feel like to see a laughingstock franchise transformed into consistent winners, thanks to sound baseball operating principles. I'd seen it happen, up close, to my close friends who loved the Boston Red Sox. If Theo Epstein could do it in Boston, I knew I could do it in New York. And I didn't think it would take new ownership, either, the way it had for the Red Sox. It would just take some convincing.

Chapter 6

THE WILLIAM JENNINGS BRYAN
OF BASEBALL FANS

I N   T H E   F A L L of 2001, I was reading quietly in my Bard
College dorm room when I heard a knock at the door. Nick
van der Kolk, a freshman living in my building who'd dis-
closed an affinity for the Boston Red Sox in a few brief conversations, had printed out a roster.

"Let's fix the Red Sox," he said hopefully. I invited him in to
do just that, and he became one of my closest college friends.

A year later, I sent a casual e-mail to an international-
relations writer for a publication I was editing at that time, letting him know that the upcoming issue was going to be devoted
solely to baseball and that for the moment his services wouldn't
be needed. He asked if he could participate, since he knew
more about baseball than international relations.

With that, Konstantin "Kostya" Medvedovsky became a
constant companion, usually for marathon sessions of Baseball
Mogul, a computer simulation that allows you to take control
of any major-league franchise in any year.

I was working evenings at a newspaper near the Bard campus, so on a regular basis, Kostya would get into my car around

twelve thirty A.M. and return to campus around seven thirty for his early-morning classes. Rumors quickly began swirling that he had joined the CIA—a far more plausible argument, I suppose, than the idea that he'd spent the evening simulating the Boston Red Sox many years into the future.

Both Kostya, a native of Newton, Massachusetts, and Nick, from the South End of Boston, came to their love of baseball in different ways than I had. Nick, the son of a therapist, and Kostya, whose parents were computer scientists, both received little in the way of baseball instruction from immigrant parents unschooled in the American game.

But both of them adored the Boston Red Sox. And in November of 2002 they were given a gift I desperately wanted the New York Mets to have.

New owners John Henry and Larry Lucchino hired twenty-eight-year-old Theo Epstein to be the new general manager that November, to general snickering from the industry at large. The *New York Times* headline sounds almost incredulous: RED SOX ARE SAID TO NAME A 28-YEAR-OLD AS GENERAL MANAGER.

What became clear almost immediately was that the Boston Red Sox were immediately set to wrest the mantle of the stat lover's favorite team from the Oakland Athletics. (A year later, perhaps as a comeback, the A's were chronicled in Michael Lewis's bestselling book *Moneyball*.) Within two weeks of Epstein's hiring, he'd acquired one person who would come to define the Epstein-era Red Sox: Bill James.

To understand what this meant to us—a bunch of stat geeks living in upstate New York—and to the baseball world at large, it is necessary to understand precisely who Bill James is, both from an intellectual and chronological perspective. James began writing about baseball with the idea that conventional

wisdom—on bunting, on relief pitching, on the value of batting average, and many other topics—could and should be tested
using all available information. He coined the term *sabermetrics*
as a catchall term for this mode of thinking, after the Society
for American Baseball Research (SABR—get it?), a group of
baseball writers and historians.

James's rise to prominence is a Horatio Alger–like story. His
first annual study of baseball, in 1977, was compiled while he
worked nights as a security guard for a grain silo. He sold somewhere around one hundred copies of a booklet he put together
and mailed himself.

But as his ideas slowly drew more notice, he became more
and more popular, and by the mid-1980s his annuals were required reading for thinking baseball fans. So for those who'd
already formed their opinions about baseball, or were unwilling to consider alternate points of view, James could be easily
dismissed. But for a new generation of fans, his work caught
on in much the same way that children introduced to foreign
languages achieve fluency far more easily than adults do. I'd
received my copy of *The Bill James Historical Baseball Abstract* as
a Hanukkah present in 1987, at age seven.

Theo Epstein, it is worth noting, is just six years older than I
am. He grew up in a very Bill James world, too. It was also a
very Red Sox world, just a few blocks from Fenway Park. He'd
grown up dreaming of ending Boston's infamous championship
drought, not by making a diving catch in center field or throwing a back-breaking curveball, but by building a well-planned,
deep, and devastatingly talented roster and watching his players
go to work.

It's not that folks like Epstein and I didn't enjoy playing the
game—we did. My intramural softball team never lacked for

enthusiasm, though winning was not a regular part of our routine. And once I discovered a batting cage just twenty minutes away, we'd pile into my Nissan and travel along Route 9G, past family farms and Happy Clown Ice Cream, to hit baseballs at fifty cents per twenty pitches late into the evening.

But building a team produced something as beautiful as watching one of those line drives rifle off my bat, ring delightfully against the pitching machine, or take off into the netting while we pictured it continuing its journey into the rural evening landscape. Baseball rosters were a puzzle, and I was getting good at finding solutions. Finding that perfect right-handed first baseman to platoon with the lefty who couldn't hit southpaws, seeing the ideal bullpen complement pop up on the waiver wire, watching that top draft pick begin to absolutely rake at Triple-A, knowing his big-league debut draws near . . . it's as satisfying as completing a crossword puzzle, putting the last piece into a jigsaw, anything like that.

Except it's better. Once you've finished that crossword puzzle, it doesn't play 162 games of the finest sport ever devised.

As the 2003 season got under way, the Red Sox appeared to be very different from their predecessors. When Nick knocked on my door, the Red Sox weren't very different from the 2010 Mets. The team had struggled to roughly a .500 finish, had reached the playoffs three times in the past eleven years. But they'd also managed to waste a pair of MVP-caliber seasons from Mo Vaughn, some of the finest years any shortstop had ever played from Nomar Garciaparra, and the best four years of any starting pitcher in major-league history, Pedro Martinez. Like the Mets of Reyes, Wright, Santana, and Beltran, the Red Sox hadn't managed to secure even a single World Series appearance with that talent, let alone a championship.

This 2003 team was put together differently. Bill Mueller, a third baseman who would go on to hit .326 that year, leading the American League, signed for just $4.2 million over two years. First baseman Kevin Millar, purchased from the Marlins in February 2003 and earning just $2 million himself, would hit 25 home runs. And most famously, David Ortiz would hit 31 home runs and slug .592, all for the meager sum of $1.25 million after the Minnesota Twins released him.

In other words, the Red Sox weren't just relying on their big-ticket items anymore. Taking a chance on secondary players with upside, identifying players other teams hadn't properly valued, and building a roster that fit together was the new Boston Red Sox way.

While Nick and Kostya experienced this renaissance, I lived through the 2003 Mets, who were, at least, consistent: Their big-name players were as bad as the guys they added on the cheap. An injury to Mike Piazza signaled the beginning of the end. (Piazza, treated as Mets typically were, was moved to first base during the regular season with no warning, hearing about the move through the press, befitting the unplanned nature of so much the Mets did.) Roberto Alomar performed the way Annie Hall did the time Alvy asked her to make love without getting high. Tom Glavine, who'd tormented the Mets as a member of the Braves for years, signed just as the umps stopped giving him a strike on his notorious pitch a few inches off the outside of the plate. He wound up with a 4.52 ERA.

I still had my favorites, naturally, from begoggled catcher and first baseman Jason Phillips to Korean sensation Jae Weong Seo, who rode two pitches to a respectable 3.82 ERA in the rotation. And a twenty-year-old Jose Reyes immediately became must-stop-and-watch viewing. But when the Mets' season mercifully ended (they were 66–95), I found I had somewhere else to turn: the most compelling baseball team I'd ever adopted stood ready to challenge the Yankees in the postseason.

Without a dog of my own in the fight, I had any number of reasons to support the Boston Red Sox. They were the bitter enemies of the New York Yankees, meaning a Boston victory over New York in the playoffs would resonate like nothing else in the empty area where Yankees fans were supposed to have souls. (This was a reality that Mets fans, as crosstown rivals of the Yankees, were all too familiar with.) Plus the Red Sox, from a Mets perspective, had provided the greatest memory of my childhood in the person of Bill Buckner. As someone who rooted for the underdog, I still felt a little guilty about that.

Two of my closest friends were long-suffering Red Sox fans. Their general manager adhered to Jamesian principles, meaning that the success of the Red Sox could convince other teams to adopt similar principles. (The Mets, for example.) Their general manager's father, Leslie Epstein, was one of my literary heroes. Their general manager's grandfather and great-uncle, Philip and Julius Epstein, wrote great films, including *Casablanca*, among my favorites.

Did I mention how upset Yankees fans would be to lose to the Red Sox?

A few things surprised me about rooting for the Red Sox in the postseason, however. For one thing, I really cared if they won or lost. Not the way I did about the Mets, of course—of course!—but still, I discovered that it actually mattered to me. Driving home from Yom Kippur in South Jersey, I hit the steering wheel in excitement, emitting a short blast from my horn, when Derek Lowe recorded the final out of the ALDS, drawing an angry look from the man stuck in New Jersey Turnpike traffic just ahead of me.

The other thing I found surprising was how hard it was to convince both Nick and Kostya that winning the World Series would be entirely possible for the Red Sox. Neither had the capacity to really believe this. And I think it came directly from the fundamental difference between how the Mets fan and the Red Sox fan each interpreted history.

For the Mets fan, losing was the natural order of things. Still, when the stars aligned to produce a good or great Mets team, they really aligned. So you saw miracles like 1969, or the 1973 pennant for a team that found itself in last place in August, or a series of comeback victories in the 1986 playoffs, punctuated by that Game 6 World Series return from the last rites. (And don't forget, the Mets trailed Boston 3–0 in Game 7 as well.)

For the Red Sox, seeing the team do well was par for the course. The Red Sox posted winning records in thirteen of eighteen seasons from 1986 through 2003. But when they got close to the prize, something always got in the way—Enos Slaughter in 1946, Bob Gibson in 1967, the Cincinnati Reds in 1975, themselves in 1986. The Yankees in 1949, the Yankees in 1978, the Yankees year after year after year. And the Yankees stood ready to do it again in the American League Championship Series.

The series couldn't have been closer. The two teams split the first six games, including a pair of one-run decisions, and the Red Sox tied the series at 3–3 with an epic comeback at Yankee Stadium to force a Game 7. It just so happened that Thursday was my night off, so I drove over to North Campus at Bard, where Nick, Kostya, and about a dozen other baseball fans had crowded in front of the second-largest television at the college to watch baseball history.

The three of us grabbed dinner at a nearby diner in Kingston, and I vividly remember trying to convince them both that there was no earthly reason why Boston couldn't win. Sure, the Yankees had won 101 games, but the Sox had 95 wins of their own—far from shabby. Anything could happen in a seven-game series. New York's ace, Roger Clemens, had a fine year, with a 3.91 ERA, but Pedro Martinez had another utterly dominant year, with a 2.22 ERA. The two teams had played twenty-five times that season; Boston had won thirteen of those contests.

Still, when it came to Game 7, both Nick and Kostya were sure something terrible was about to happen, while I believed the Yankee tyranny over Boston would end that very night. So what happened next was heartbreaking. When the Red Sox took a 3–0 lead, I could see Kostya and Nick begin to believe that fate had in fact taken a new direction for their team. I knew they were making the same calculations I was with each passing out, that the percentage chance of victory was growing.

Nick was a jumble of emotions, bouncing around the room, never sitting anywhere for very long. Neither Kostya nor I moved, providing a reminder that superstition in baseball exists for even the sabermetrically inclined. It makes sense, too: The Red Sox had outscored the Yankees 5–2 while I'd been in that particular chair. (Small sample size was ignored for the moment.)

What happened next, of course, has been immortalized many times over. Red Sox manager Grady Little, with a tiring Pedro on the mound and a 5–2 lead in the eighth inning, let the Yankees tie the game against his spent pitcher rather than summon one of his effective relievers. The Yankees fans in the room, largely silent all night, would later claim simple quiet confidence that turned to jeers directed at those who supported Boston. When Jorge Posada's bloop double fell in front of Johnny Damon, tying the game at 5, Kostya took off out of the room. As he told me later, "I knew what would happen next."

What happened next, three innings later, was Aaron Boone's home run into the left-field seats off Tim Wakefield, sending the Yankees to the World Series. Again. As Nick put it when we repaired to that same diner, just the two of us: "Of course it had to be Wakefield. The ultimate Red Sox guy." He'd been with Boston since 1995. He'd thrown thousands of knuckle-balls to induce thousands of outs. But his first one to Boone stayed straight. Such is the limit of stats and probability to in-fluence a single event. It's precisely what makes a game with so many useful numbers so great: For all the analysis made possi-ble by the numbers, the game consistently surprises with indi-vidual plays. Over long seasons, the knowledge provided by advanced statistical analysis will make your team better. And yet, baseball is most thrilling when the unlikely occurs—as it so frequently does.

In the year following that painful loss, much had happened. The Mets had made fools of those who believed in their early-season success, much as they did in 2010. The trade of Scott Kazmir for Victor Zambrano, now notorious in Mets folklore, provided a grim reminder of how wide the gap was between the manage-ment of the Mets and not only the Red Sox, but even the Devil Rays. (I'll come to my own thoughts on trading pitching pros-pects later.)

It had taken a few days for Kostya and Nick to get over that

Game 7 loss. Even our nonbaseball interaction suffered; it seemed as if they blamed me, at some level, for allowing them to believe toppling the Yankees could happen. Meanwhile, I was surer than ever that Boston's glass ceiling had been cracked, and a few more moves would allow them to vanquish the Yankees at long last.

But what would that mean to me? For all the struggles of the New York Mets, I walked out of my final regular-season game at Shea that year—a 4–2 loss to the Expos on the final Friday night of the season—sadder than I'd been after Game 7 of the 2003 ALCS. All the logical reasons in the world pointed to jumping on the Boston bandwagon—it was a team that practiced the things I, a future GM candidate, had been preaching for years. But there was a limit to what they could mean to me, because, let's face it: They weren't the Mets.

Still, it was exciting to see the Red Sox acquire Curt Schilling, and during the 2004 season to watch the Greek God of Walks, Kevin Youkilis, make a significant contribution; to experience Mark Bellhorn finally getting regular at-bats at second base (and prove his sabermetric supporters right). To see Theo Epstein deal Nomar Garciaparra as part of a complicated trade-deadline deal on July 31 was to see a new breed of general manager at the height of his powers. So when Boston entered the playoffs with a better runs scored/runs allowed mark than the Yankees, along with two pitchers in Pedro and Schilling better than anything the Yankees had, it was hard not to be confident.

Unless, of course, you were Nick or Kostya. We made the decision to split up while watching the first few games of the series, even when I had days off, not wanting any part of the 2003 Game 7 experience to repeat itself. Like I said, we were stat people, and the stats told us that heartbreak happened when we watched together.

No matter: It appeared I'd see the Yankees clinch in Game 4 from the comfort of the newsroom, anyway. By October 2004, I'd been promoted to sports editor at the *Hudson Register-Star*; it was my job to write a column about the game when it concluded. So as Game 4 reached what looked to be the final innings with the Yankees up a run and set to sweep, I knew I didn't want to be in a newsroom filled with Yankees fans.

I walked down the stairs of the roughly two-hundred-year-old building and headed out to my car to listen to what I assumed would be Mariano Rivera closing out the Red Sox. The *Register-Star* building was once a jail, with the only public hanging in Hudson history taking place in a courtyard right in front of the well-preserved structure. I walked to my car, parked across the street, and looked at the scene, knowing I was listening to another execution, 170 years later.

But as most baseball fans know, fate finally, mercifully, gave the Red Sox a full and complete pardon. Kevin Millar singled. Dave Roberts pinch-ran, stole second base, and came around to score on a single by Bill Mueller. The Great Rivera had been bested, and Game 4 continued. I returned to the office and continued watching, with those from the newsroom joining the crowd. The game continued deep into the night; no one left.

And so began the most dramatic baseball experience of my life that didn't involve the Mets. For the next three innings, I knew any scoring from the Yankees could end the improbable Boston comeback. With one outburst, a team that had battered Boston pitching for 19 runs in Game 3 alone could stop this series cold. The Yankees put the leadoff hitter on in the eleventh, in the twelfth—they came up empty both times, leaving the bases loaded in the eleventh.

The reactions in the newsroom when David Ortiz hit a two-run homer, sending the series to a Game 5, were notable. A member of Red Sox Nation, a fan of the Minnesota Twins, and me, a Mets fan through and through, all celebrated together. The Yankees fans went on their way, content in knowing how this struggle turns out in the end. I exultantly started writing the column I'd held the sports section back for, easily composing despite the late hour.

Less than twenty-four hours after the five-hour-and-two-minute Game 4 ended, Game 5 began—and this time, the action lasted five hours and forty-nine minutes, fourteen innings of tightrope navigation. I had the night off, and Nick, Kostya, and I found a common area at Bard to watch the game—making sure to pick a different one from the 2003 room. To be extrasafe, we went to a different part of the campus, a short but important walk down the road.

But more than just the location resonated differently with all of us this time. There was no convincing Nick and Kostya that the Red Sox could advance—we all knew no baseball team had ever recovered from a 3–0 deficit to win a seven-game series. This was new territory for the Red Sox—to find themselves in a position where losing would be expected and winning would be what shocked the baseball world.

It felt very much like rooting for the New York Mets.

And I have talked to so many Mets fans since then who felt as I did. Who came away from those nearly six-hour games emotionally wrung-out. Who exulted when Tom Gordon coughed up a 4–2 lead in the eighth inning, when Jason Varitek calmly lifted a sac fly to center off of the Great Rivera—of course Rivera would blow two saves in twenty-four hours! Things had changed. I told Nick and Kostya about what had been the best first date of my life. Everything seemed possible.

I returned to work for Game 6, now better known as the Bloody Sock Game. However, I'd done something new to augment the occasion. I purchased a Boston Red Sox shirt.

This was new territory for me. I'd had occasion to own articles of clothing belonging to other major-league teams growing up, usually gifts from nonspecific friends or relatives. I still remembered attending a Bar Mitzvah in a luxury box at Veterans Stadium in Philadelphia and receiving a Phillies hat as a parting gift. What should I do with such an unpleasant reminder of that team the Mets played? It didn't look right anywhere in my room, the tacky red clashing with my sea of orange and blue. I finally placed it deep in my closet, under my least-worn clothing. I assume it is still there.

But I drove into Kingston, found the Red Sox apparel next to the mountain of Yankee goods, and purchased a simple navy T-shirt with three buttons to simulate a professional uniform, the stitched Red Sox letters in scarlet adorning the front. It felt foreign in my hands, and I wondered, not for the first time, how my allegiances would reorient when this postseason journey ended.

Naturally, the bloody-sock game provided more column inches for me—another reason to root for the Red Sox—and I started my Game 7 column once the Red Sox took an 8–1 lead in the fourth inning. After I put the paper to bed, I sought out Nick and Kostya, and we celebrated. The team we'd started to put together ourselves on the pad Nick brought to my dorm room in 2001—and perfected deep into the nights on a lone computer in Dutchess County—had been created by Theo Epstein and had vanquished the Yankees.

What followed was arguably the dullest World Series of my lifetime. I certainly enjoyed seeing Boston finally win, ending the misery of numerous long-suffering fans, among them my two friends. But after the climactic ALCS, there was little drama left to this story.

I did permit myself one final bit of schadenfreude. Once the Red Sox beat the Yankees, I thought it only appropriate to localize the story—journey to the local sporting-goods stores, bars, and other stores in search of people wearing Yankee or Red Sox hats and get their take on the historic series. It was difficult to keep a completely serious face when asking someone in a Yankee hat, "So when exactly did you know you were watching the biggest collapse in baseball history?" To be on the safe side, I made certain to get more quotes than I'd possibly need—just to be diligent. Knowing he was a Yankees fan, I even called the mayor.

I still have that Boston T-shirt, but it's buried beneath my mountain of Mets shirts—the player-jersey knockoffs of Jose Reyes, Carlos Beltran, and even Mo Vaughn and Kaz Matsui, the NL East Champions shirt I purchased from a Shea vendor in the upper reserved just after seeing the team clinch, even the 2006 NL Champions shirt I bought for five dollars from a knockoff vendor on my way to the car after the Mets fell one game short of accomplishing what the T-shirt proclaimed.

Nick and Kostya went to the parade in Boston, but I knew it wasn't my place, and I would have felt strange being there. The pleasures attendant in seeing the team you've followed so closely, season after season, cannot be replicated without actually following that team closely, season after season. The players on the Red Sox hadn't been in my living room night after night. Their predecessors hadn't been the stars of the stories I'd grown up reading or hearing from my father. So there was also a certain pain that came with Boston's victory, as I imagined William Jennings Bryan felt each of the three times he was nominated for president, but lost—the chance to stand close to someone whose lifelong dreams were realized. And the Mets, my Mets, seemed so far from this precipice. Alhough at first blush it sounds like a valid comparison, there was nothing adulterous about my two-month tryst with the Red Sox. Scott Kazmir for Victor Zambrano had made us all feel like widowers.

And by 2005, the Red Sox were just another team again—one I had affection for, but not one I felt compelled to follow on a regular basis. Instead, what I learned from the experience of the 2003 and 2004 playoffs was what it felt like to have your hopes first raised, then dashed, then insulted, and then, miraculously, realized. From where I sit now, it feels like nothing less than foreshadowing for what the Mets put us through from 2007 to 2010, some of the darkest days of the franchise. And now, I was hoping, deliverance was near.

I learned that cursed franchises need only competent management, especially in big markets, to become successful franchises. Boston didn't outspend the Yankees—David Ortiz made $4.5 million in 2004, or one fifth as much as Alex Rodriguez. Moreover, Theo Epstein picked him up for nothing. And in ripples of roster moves, Epstein did the same thing, again and again, to supplement his stars and build a champion.

By November, however, I was spending much of my time hoping the Mets could steal Pedro Martinez away from those very same Red Sox. That first date with Rachel turned into a second date, a third date, and within a few weeks, it was Rachel who was forced to listen to the way I could fashion the New York Mets into a Boston Red Sox–type champion—which still felt odd to say. By April, it was baseball season—Mets season—and Rachel and I were engaged. Five years later, it was Rachel who cast the very first vote in the initial Howard Megdal for general manager primary.

Chapter 7

THE PEOPLE BEGIN TO SPEAK

A N AL GM told ESPN.com's Buster Olney that he believes the Twins could acquire Lee with a package built around prospect Wilson Ramos," I cooed softly as I rocked Mirabelle in our glider, the voices of Howie Rose and Wayne Hagin describing the action of a Mets game against the Marlins in the background of the darkened nursery room. "Rival GMs believe the Rangers may be better off holding on to their prospects than acquiring Lee."

As my daughter turned three months old, a routine had developed around the Megdal household. My wife, a teacher off until September, watched Mirabelle for much of the day while I worked on my writing and the campaign. In the evenings, I gave Mirabelle her final bottle of the night and put her to sleep with a combination of Mets games on the radio, notable news stories (with annotated comments from me), and MLB Trade Rumors updates (with player background also supplied by me).

Mirabelle and I began watching more games, but the late innings tended to fall after her bedtime. So I viewed this time in her life as the period when she could get critical background information for the times she'd eventually watch full games.

"The Mariners will require a blue-chip prospect in a Cliff Lee trade, reports Joel Sherman of the *New York Post*, even though the last two Lee trades may not have included one," I explained to Mirabelle, reading Tim Dierkes's post. "Sherman suggests the Mets want Lee badly, while the Yankees would just like the M's to 'keep them posted.'"

I liked our pediatrician, but she'd infuriated me with her medical advice about when it would be safe to take Mirabelle to a Mets game. Somehow her baby naming, at a synagogue surrounded by people who could have colds, the flu, or plague, was just fine at eight weeks of age. But it would be best to wait "as long as possible" to bring Mirabelle to Citi Field, she said, due to the issue of germs.

I chose not to make an issue of it. I didn't want our doctor to think I was questioning her expertise and decide to, say, replace Mirabelle's MMR shot with Sanka. But I also knew that this simply could not stand. Citi Field was a clean place; it wasn't as if I'd be taking Mirabelle to Shea Stadium. It was newer than our synagogue. It had more fresh air than the doctor's office. And it was more sacred than . . . anything, really.

In the words of W. P. Kinsella, "A ballpark at night is more like a church than a church."

Rachel and I had a Saturday-plan ticket pack, meaning that fifteen games per season we made the pilgrimage to Citi Field, in addition to the many non–Saturday games I covered as a columnist. That represented far more time than our treks to synagogue, where we had the popular Reform Judaism Two Dates and a Guilt Complex plan, in which we attended Rosh Hashanah, Yom Kippur, and felt badly numerous other times about not attending.

"Sherman explains that the Mariners like, but don't love, Mets pitching prospect Jenrry Mejia," I read to Mirabelle. "He feels that a Mets trade would have to be built around Mejia or Wilmer Flores."

I took the doctor's orders at face value. "As long as possible" wouldn't be for very much longer. I'd done due diligence for recalls on every single item we'd bought her; I relentlessly cleaned her orthodontic-approved pacifiers; but at a certain point, life intervened. Taking my daughter to Mets games was non-negotiable. Naturally, Rachel was on board for this as well, and we began the process of finding a night that would work best. In the meantime, it was left to Howie Rose, Wayne Hagin, and me to prepare Mirabelle for her life as a Mets fan.

A single by Rod Barajas and a double by Chris Carter brought Jeff Francoeur to the plate in the top of the ninth inning, the Marlins ahead 6–4. "Chances are the Marlins couldn't walk Francoeur here, even if they tried to give him an intentional pass," I explained to Mirabelle. Sure enough, on the first pitch, Francoeur grounded out to the second baseman. "One of the reasons I'm running for GM is so that by the time you are old enough to remember things, players like Jeff Francoeur won't be Mets anymore."

Josh Thole followed with a single to tie the game, and I told Mirabelle about how useful a player like Thole could be in assembling a roster. "Having Thole in the everyday lineup would mean paying the major-league minimum to one of your starting players," I said as Mirabelle made it clear she understood by absently reaching for my chin. "Thole wouldn't even be eligible for arbitration for several years, giving the Mets payroll flexibility during that entire period of time. And Thole could be a productive starting catcher immediately."

It seemed that the Zen qualities inherent in a low-cost everyday player had finally lulled Mirabelle to sleep. Normally we'd feed for about an inning, I'd read to her for another inning, and she was asleep somewhere between the fourth and sixth, depending on the quality of pitching that night. For whatever reason, we'd been at this into the ninth inning, and roughly three minutes after I'd put her in the crib, I heard her cry out again. Was she desperate for resolution in a 6–6 game?

"The ninth inning will be difficult to navigate," I said to Mirabelle as I calmed her on my shoulder, soothing her with back caresses. "The Mets have used both Bobby Parnell and K-Rod, and Florida has right-handed hitters coming up."

We settled back into the glider and heard lefty Pedro Feliciano give up the game to a double by Jorge Cantu and a single by Dan Uggla, righties both. "It's hard to blame Jerry Manuel for this one," I told Mirabelle. "He really didn't have any other options to use there."

With the game over, I checked through the dim light to see if Mirabelle showed the customary signs of impending sleep— heavy eyelids, the hand to her face. Not tonight. I had a smiling baby on my hands, and even her feet were somewhat active. The truth was, I didn't mind this a bit—it meant I got to keep talking to her.

There was, after all, a lot of catching up to do.

"The voting started this week in my run for GM," I explained to the smiling baby, deciding to give her a few more days before I explained representative democracy, the party system, or how you could have a primary for a nongovernment management job. "It's looking good for Daddy right now, but the totals are still very close in both primaries. We need to hope that all my voters haven't turned out already."

The voting had started on two of the eighteen blogs I'd included in my effort to show the Wilpons that my message of LOGIC, TRANSPARENCY, and PASSION had broad-based appeal. I'd chosen the first few blogs especially to indicate that I could reach Mets fans of very different stripes.

For the week of June 28 to July 2, voting took place at Amazin' Avenue and Mike Silva's New York Baseball Digest. These were arguably the two most diametrically opposed Mets sites around, if that was possible with two blogs about the Mets. You'd be surprised how much argument two sites like this could generate. (Unless, you know, you're one of the people who does the arguing.) As should be clear by now, very few people take the Mets more seriously than I do. But clearly there are some.

Amazin' Avenue represents some of the most logical thinking available on the Internet about any baseball team, and certainly the New York Mets. This sabermetrically inspired blog had long affirmed many of the basic tenets I carried forth into my baseball writing and hoped to take into the office of general manager. The editor, Eric Simon, had been publishing my poems recapping every single Mets game since 2007. But that didn't mean I always agreed with him, and some of the writers over at AA refused to brook disagreement in a convivial way. This never made a bit of sense to me: One of the great things about baseball arguments is we can watch the players settle them on the field. But clearly there were folks who felt otherwise and weren't afraid to say so.

Often, that abuse was directed at Mike Silva. I'd also known Mike for some time and had written for him since 2007 as

well. And it wouldn't be fair to say that Mike was anti-stats—
baseball *is* stats, and stats are baseball. But Mike enjoyed having alternate viewpoints on his site and would frequently invite
me to immediately write a piece disagreeing with him when I
did. Mike's site is where I wrote about Rod Barajas—and heard
about it from readers.

Naturally, simply agreeing to disagree wasn't far enough. The
same writer for AA who promised to "put down and bury" my
GM run had repeatedly called on me to disassociate myself from
Mike's site. It seemed pretty obvious that my refusal to do so had
fueled his attempts to sabotage the campaign, as I explained to
Rachel when she read some of his comments. I reminded her that
this was the same person who'd e-mailed me during our Florida
vacation back in 2009, repeatedly referring to Mike, in decidedly
nonsabermetric terms, as an "ass clown."

"So he's upset because you agree with Mike?"

"No, that I continue to write for Mike's site even when I
don't agree with him."

"But Mike lets you write whatever you want. You usually
disagree with him on the air, and he's so nice about it!" Mike
and I often disagreed on our weekly radio show.

"I know."

"So what exactly is the problem?"

"It's kind of a holy war for some people."

The war in question has been around for a good twenty-five
years and may as well have been started by Bill James: the feud
between received wisdom and statistical analysis. Anyone who'd
read a few words of my writing knew where I stood: For measuring performance, there was nothing better than stats, though
obviously, contrary to the stereotype (and reality) of statheads, I

believed in watching the games. If I didn't believe this all the way down to my core, well, then I wouldn't be running for GM.

But clearly if I couldn't find a way to tailor my message to both sides of what had become a huge battlefield throughout baseball, I wouldn't make for much of a communicator—one of the most important aspects to the job of general manager.

The way I looked at it, we analytical types weren't doing anything so very different. Baseball, for one thing, has always been about numbers. Ted Williams batted .406. Babe Ruth hit 714 homers. Roger Maris hit 61 in a season—with an asterisk. These numbers were seared into the brains of every baseball fan—so much so that, when it turned out that Mark McGwire broke Maris's record under dubious circumstances, the United States government felt obliged to get involved. Is there another number, in all of American history, that's so sacred?

And when you look at it that way, what was so wrong with measuring not just home runs and RBI but walks, on-base average, defense, runs created, slugging percentage? Every other discipline in science, economics, and technology had evolved since Babe Ruth's era—why not baseball too?

More than that, you had to appreciate where baseball geeks like myself were coming from. When you think like me, and you really love something, what you do is study it. No one has a problem with marine biologists, philosophers, or architects who do this. And baseball, although it takes extraordinary toughness, athleticism, and skill to play, can be understood by anyone. This was the whole point of my candidacy: Pursue the things you love. If you dream of one day building the perfect baseball team and you believe you have the tools to do it? Well, then it's crazy *not* to stage a fake primary on a Web site.

I also happened to believe the gap between the two camps was far smaller than was generally acknowledged.

The stereotype of the sabermetric view of baseball usually portrayed someone who didn't watch the games. In my years writing about baseball, I'd encountered many fans and observers who relied on stats to a significant extent to contextualize what they were, yes, watching. I'd honestly not met a single person who enjoyed calculating various degrees of mathematical formulas to further our understanding of baseball yet didn't love watching a baseball game. Frankly, I've found that people within the sabermetrics movement tend to be more interested in watching games than the writers in the media who take pleasure in stereotyping them.

By contrast, the number of media members who refuse to consider any of the statistical advances made in the past few decades are increasingly rare. Sure, even a saber-friendly journalist will occasionally misinterpret some new stat, but that's just a writer trying to speak French, not a reason to disparage all French people. The other part of the equation to consider is that for many baseball observers, the value of a player isn't taken through just statistical evidence. Now, for me, finding statistics that weed out much of the noise inherent in our own observations is crucial and takes precedent. But something I love about baseball is that reasonable people can disagree on how much to weigh various kinds of evidence.

So as the election began in earnest, I knew that my refusal to create an electrified fence between my work and that of people who took a different view had inspired an opposition in, of all places, a group that would run the Mets pretty much as I would if given the chance. But I also believed that among the thousands of Amazin' Avenue readers, just as with most of their writers, there were many who could do more than rally around a negative point of view: They could embrace a positive call for specific change. I didn't believe for a second that readers flocked to Amazin' Avenue, or New York Baseball Digest, or read my work, simply to get angry. I'd met or heard from too many readers who took pleasure in the silly rhymes of the daily Mets poetry, whose love for the team was the driving force behind their relentless fandom, and who didn't use the relative distance of the Internet as an excuse for abusing those who disagreed with them. Those people would surely vote for me, no?

The polls, however, would determine if I was right.

And so began a week of constant motion. During the day, I made phone calls to shore up support for future primaries. I wrote for all my usual outlets, from SNY.tv to MLBTradeRumors.com to New York Baseball Digest. I grabbed every window I could for a little playtime with Mirabelle. But I couldn't help myself—my fate was being decided at both Amazin' Avenue and New York Baseball Digest. It felt as if my entire career to date was up for referendum.

The early voting on both sites was tight. I'd e-mailed my friends and family, but the Mets fans only—I wanted this to be a vote among the fan base itself. And the frustration of an Internet campaign, naturally, is that all the typical outlets available to someone running for office—going door-to-door, making phone calls, campaigning in person—aren't really available. Even the Mets were out of town, making a Citi Field appearance to round up votes impossible. I'd rise or fall on the strength of my ideas.

In the meantime, the reviews continued to come in. Will Leitch of *New York* magazine referred to my run in a piece entitled "The Mets Are the Hottest Team in Baseball," calling me a "Mets gadfly and poet," not without a note of dismissal. As Leitch concluded, "His timing couldn't be worse: The Mets are so hot right now, even Omar Minaya looks smart." Of course, he'd written three weeks earlier of the same Mets: "This is an organization collapsing on itself . . . this Mets season has been riddled with head-scratching moves that bespeak an organization without direction."

Steve Keane at the Eddie Kranepool Society was far more supportive, putting the hot streak of June into perspective: "None of those men have put in the time, effort and passion into the New York Mets like Howard Megdal has . . . Howard Megdal has put aside his writing and broadcasting career to run for GM of the Mets to restore what is missing from this organization, which has lost it way. Do not let this recent run of prosperity sway your thinking. Howard will restore everything that has been missing for years in the Met front office, LOGIC, TRANSPARENCY, PASSION."

And Josh Alper of NBC New York took a more analytical view:

Some might say that Megdal's mission is misguided. The Mets' general manager is not selected by the voters, of course. That is probably for the best in the long run, although the world would probably be a more amusing place if the public got to make such choices. The other reason why some might argue that Megdal is barking up the wrong tree is that the Mets are actually winning more often than they lose right now.

In this space and others, the return of winning has led to some complimentary words for the recent personnel move made by Omar Minaya and the rest of the front office. The promotion of Ike Davis, turfing of Gary Matthews Jr. and whole-scale reinvention of the starting rotation are the things cited most often and there's even been some kudos tossed in Minaya's direction for finally pulling the plug on Jennry Mejia's stint in the major leagues.

Megdal's commercial gets you thinking, though: Is it really commendable to correct mistakes that everyone but you knew were mistakes from the get-go?

. . . The bar is really low when we're willing to accept realizing that you've made a mistake—not admitting it nor learning from it, simply realizing it—as a sign of growth.

So, clearly, some people got it. Some people didn't. And some people didn't want to get it. But the larger goal was intact: People were looking at the New York Mets in a longer-term context, and envisioning how different the future could be with a different set of guiding principles for the ballclub. I spent the week continuing to speak to a new set of ideas.

And I continued to hit refresh on two open browser windows. The voting was pretty tight early in the week, around fifty-fifty in both places. But as the week went on, something miraculous began to happen. My voters kept on showing up.

As the vote totals climbed into the hundreds, and eventually over a thousand at each site, my lead began to increase. I went to bed on Tuesday night at 51 percent at Amazin' Avenue, 52 percent at NYBD; by the morning I'd improved to 55 percent at each site. I was overjoyed to discover that I'd done more than just earn a living by writing about the Mets. Clearly, I'd communicated a positive vision for the team that had people responding.

As the week went on, the numbers kept climbing, By Thursday, I was over 60 percent in both votes, by Friday up around 65 percent. The final totals had me at 65 percent in Amazin' Avenue, 68 percent at New York Baseball Digest. The people had begun to speak. And at the risk of channeling Richard Nixon, the noise from a few had been drowned out by a silent majority that saw my campaign as a path to a better Mets tomorrow. I won't lie: It was gratifying. This, after all, was my career: Having ideas about the Mets and interacting with people was what I did for a living. Not only did it earn me a pretty decent living, but it was a profession I chose out of passion. To hear people embrace me as a thoughtful and trustworthy critic—really, it meant a lot. And maybe even more to the point, it represented the best evidence yet that all Mets fans really wanted was some competence. It was well known that in recent years, Mets fans had been relentlessly negative. But this was no permanent state of mind, just a reaction to recent events. We just needed change we could believe in!

I wrote a heartfelt thank-you to my supporters before our Chinese food arrived and Rachel, Mirabelle, and I watched the Mets game on television. It was hard to overstate my feeling of empowerment about the future:

> The first two primary votes are now complete. And despite competing simultaneously at both New York Baseball Digest and Amazin' Avenue, a pair of sites often diametrically opposed in viewpoints, I am humbled to have received a strong mandate from both sets of readers.
>
> Over at Amazin' Avenue, with immense interest and participation, I have captured 65 percent of the vote. At New York Baseball Digest, the mandate is even more overwhelming: a whopping 68 percent of the vote.

To put this in perspective, let's look at some of the biggest landslides in political history:

Candidate Vote %
Ronald Reagan, 1984: 58.8
Richard Nixon, 1972: 60.7
Franklin Roosevelt, 1936: 60.8
Lyndon Johnson, 1964: 61.1
Howard Megdal, AA: 65
Howard Megdal, NYBD: 68

You have voted for me because you want LOGIC, TRANSPARENCY, and PASSION on behalf of the New York Mets every single day. Facing opposition to my candidacy by those who would promote the status quo, or people who just seem to like opposing things, we have banded together to win the Iowa caucus and New Hampshire primary of my run for general manager.

As we prepare to celebrate July 4, I welcome all of you, whether you have supported my candidacy or not. I intend to be the general manager for all Mets fans, to be certain that everyone who lives and dies with the Orange and Blue has reason to celebrate, and not just on holidays or during particularly cool giveaway days.

But my work to earn the mandate of Mets fans across the world has just begun. On Monday, my next set of primaries begin, at MetsMinorLeagueBlog.com and Metsgrrl.com. I welcome the input of the literary fan one finds at Metsgrrl, thanks to the writing talent of Caryn Rose, and the system-intensive observer who reads Toby Hyde's remarkable work.

Until then, I intend to savor my victories with my wife, my daughter, and some delivery Chinese food that just arrived. Thank you for your support, and may your holiday weekend include witnessing a severe offensive beat-down of Stephen Strasburg.

And the news just kept on getting better. The mango chicken was succulent. Mirabelle went to bed early and, miraculously, let us sleep late. The Mets beat the Nationals on a pickoff play to end the game. Better still, the man picked off was Roger Bernadina, whose name was seemingly created for game-recap poetry. Like I said: I am a Mets writer.

(Sung to Mona Lisa)
Bernadina, Bernadina
Where you running?
Willie Harris, when he faces Mets, he wins
Bernadina, Bernadina
Blunder stunning
In ninth inning, simply are no greater sins
Did you try to force a balk there, Bernadina?
Or just get a healthy lead and running start?
Then Tejada snuck in right behind you
Mets had guy there
So you die there
Are you thick, are you dense, Bernadina?
Or in a loss, you simply wanted starring part

The game ended early enough for Rachel and me to watch a late movie. It felt like the first time I'd relaxed in months. The next morning, I drove to my local A&P in search of groceries. I'd decided to make dinner, and what better entree than Indian samosas? As I reached the automatic doors, I noticed the black Mets cap on the head of the teenager corralling the shopping carts, and he noticed my Mr. Met T-shirt (one of two I own). As usual, the spotting of baseball apparel acted as an entry point for discussing the Mets.

"So are we gonna get Cliff Lee?" the glasses-wearing boy with the awkward gait asked me.

"I don't know, but I'm not sure the Mets should," I responded. After all, my LOGIC, TRANSPARENCY, and PASSION had won the day with voters.

"What do you mean?" He was incredulous. "Lee's the guy they need! They aren't going anywhere without Cliff Lee."

"I just wonder how much they'll have to give up, and whether you want Lee long-term," I told him, eager to impress upon another fan the need to respect the baseball player's development curve.

"You're crazy," he said, walking back out into the parking lot, waving a dismissive hand. "This team needs Cliff Lee."

And so began a solid week of hoping, begging, praying, and cajoling from many Mets fans to acquire Cliff Lee. It was easy to understand what they were thinking: Lee was perhaps the best pitcher in all of baseball, and the Mets had big holes in their rotation. But like any candidate getting negative responses, I continued to keep my focus on the long-term mind-set. Acquiring Cliff Lee, as good as he was, would have been far more typical of the Old Regime Mets, the ones I'd been fighting so hard to change. Sure, Lee was dominant in 2010, but he was also thirty-one years old and about to hit free agency. To acquire him, the Mets would have to give up a ton of talent that could otherwise be used to help the team in 2011 and beyond—and, as previously discussed, the Mets didn't have a ton of that young talent due to the limitations of their draft strategy.

But it's awfully hard to campaign on a platform of inaction, which is what I had tried to do with the shopping-cart hauler. And it nagged at me all afternoon. While my wife and daughter napped, I meticulously wrapped the mixture of potato and pea into the phyllo dough. In the meantime, the Mets knocked the seemingly invincible Stephen Strasburg out after five innings and took a 5–2 lead into the bottom of the eighth. But in the time it took for the samosas to bake, Bobby Parnell and Francisco Rodriguez gave up the lead and Washington embarrassed the Mets on Fox's national game of the week, 6–5. The Mets lost ground to the Braves and the Phillies.

Don't get me wrong: Dinner was delicious. And Mirabelle once again went to bed early on Saturday and slept late Sunday. Rachel and I got to enjoy another movie together. But I realized that a simple Mets victory was all it took to color my Friday night in sweet pastels. And an unexpected Mets loss had taken the magic away from my hard-earned samosas.

It was yet another reminder of how powerless I was before the fortunes of the Mets. Doubtlessly, this was true for the shopping-cart maven as well. No wonder he wanted Cliff Lee! He wanted that invincible ace at the top of the rotation. Like any Mets fan thrice his age, he wanted Tom Seaver. We all did.

The trade of Seaver on June 15, 1977, was the team's version of Eve biting the apple. And both fans and the organization alike had been trying to overcome original sin ever since. Of course, employing LOGIC, TRANSPARENCY, and PASSION, the trade of Tom Seaver never would have happened.

Chapter 8

THE MALEFACTORS

HERE'S A CAMPAIGN promise for you. Read my lips: I will not accuse my team's best player of being gutless for refusing to leave via free agency. This might sound obvious to you, and it is. Unless, of course, it isn't. It has happened at least once in Mets history, and it still stands as the most egregious error committed by M. Donald Grant in what appears to be a multiyear effort to drive Tom Seaver out of town.

First, a bit about Seaver, aka the Franchise. Seaver immediately became the best pitcher on the Mets, and indeed the best pitcher they'd ever had, when he debuted in 1967. In his first season, he logged a 2.76 ERA, made the All-Star team, and was named Rookie of the Year. By any measure, he immediately placed among the best pitchers in the National League.

Consider, though, just how much his performance stood out for Mets fans. The 1967 Mets were an awful team, 61–101 on the season. And of the pitching staff, only one other pitcher besides Seaver started at least 30 games—Jack Fisher, whose ERA was nearly two runs higher at 4.70. No one else started more than 18 games, and the regular starters performed at league-average-or-below ERAs. In short, Seaver immediately presented himself to Mets fans as a savior—the one true hero of an otherwise rotten team.

The craziest part is, he got better the next year. Significantly better. As per ERA+, which measures a pitcher's ERA against the rest of the league, adjusting for park effects and era, he jumped from 122 (Hall of Fame level) to 144 (among the best ever) for the next decade. And he did it for the New York Mets. He never stopped—along with his ridiculous effectiveness, Seaver was amazingly durable. In eight of nine seasons from 1968 to 1976, he made 34 starts or more. In his injury-plagued season of 1974, that number dropped to . . . 32. The Mets cut his salary by 20 percent (the maximum decrease allowed by league rules) after the 1974 season. And Seaver, for his part, didn't complain.

But as the 1970s progressed, baseball economics experienced monumental change. The advent of free agency began to push player salaries upward. And after winning the Cy Young award in 1975, his third for the Mets, all Seaver had to do was refuse to sign his contract in 1976—it was called playing out his option—and he'd be a free agent. And considering that Catfish Hunter had signed a five-year, $3.75 million contract with the crosstown Yankees a season earlier, Seaver had to know he was in for a big payday.

But he also wanted to remain a Met. His asking price was three years, $800,000. Not because he was a poor negotiator or didn't understand the issues—Seaver remains one of the brightest men to ever don a Mets uniform, and helped lead the charge to provide players with additional bargaining rights as team union rep. No, Seaver, despite his treatment by the organization, had only ever known New York, and liked it there.

And so, through the generosity of the greatest player in their history, the Mets landed themselves three more years of stellar pitching. Three years, $675,000.

Seaver dominated again in 1976, though an increasingly poor offensive attack resulted in just 14 victories. At the beginning of 1977, the second year of his new contract, the rumors about trading Seaver began anew. Here was a pitcher, thirty-two years old, showing absolutely no signs of breaking down. He'd been their best pitcher—the best pitcher in all of baseball—over the past decade. His $675,000 deal, already very team-friendly considering his talents, was now becoming a financial relic: Following the lead of Catfish Hunter, many lesser pitchers had cashed in for more money. From a trading perspective, there may not have been another player more valuable than Seaver in all of baseball.

For the fans, trading Tom Seaver turned out to be unforgivable in retrospect. Not that the writing wasn't on the wall: The 1977 Mets weren't going to win the National League pennant; they weren't going anywhere. While no team with a modicum of a plan (or the financial resources of the Mets) has any reason to spend more than three years in rebuilding mode, Seaver, if he had to be traded, should have at least generated a haul in return to infuse the organization with young talent.

And astoundingly, the Mets had such a deal in place prior to the 1977 season. Both the Los Angeles Dodgers and Boston Red Sox were contenders in need of a frontline starter. Los Angeles had Don Sutton, but he was unhappy with his contract; and anyway, Seaver was better. The Dodgers were happy to upgrade via trade—and save money in the process. Did I mention Tom Seaver was underpaid?

The deal, as constructed, would have been a three-team, three-player swap. The Dodgers get Tom Seaver. The Red Sox get Don Sutton. The Mets get a young Jim Rice. No one would have done terribly in this swap, either. Seaver pitched to an ERA+ of 126 over his next five seasons, seldom missing a start. Sutton, durable as usual, did the same, with an ERA+ of 115. Both of them were thirty-two at the time of this deal.

But the Mets would have been the huge winner. Jim Rice was just about to turn twenty-four at the time of this potential deal. In 1977 he would go on to lead the American League in home runs with 39, then in 1978 he'd win the MVP with 46 home runs. He managed another top-five MVP vote finish over those five years, and his slash line from 1977 to 1981 checks in at .309/.362/.556. It was these years that largely propelled him into the Hall of Fame—his 142 OPS+ ranked eighth in all of baseball over those five years.

But it is the subsequent five years that really would have made this a winner for the Mets. From 1982 to his final season in 1986, Seaver pitched less than a full season twice and posted a pedestrian 105 ERA+. Sutton continued to be durable, but his ERA+ from 1982 to 1986 dipped to 103. And Rice? He just kept on hitting. Not as impressively as before, but he led the AL with 39 home runs in 1983, hit .324 in 1986, and manned left field—the one position where the Mets lacked a strong regular, even in their 1986 championship season. His 128 OPS+ still rated twenty-second in all of baseball during those five years. Of course trading Tom Seaver would have hurt. And the best strategy, when a team possesses a pitcher of Seaver's caliber, is to build around him, not decimate the major-league team and farm system to the point that trading him is the only viable option. But faced with that reality, the Mets chose not to make the deal. Then they proceeded to go out and make things much worse for themselves.

The deadline for making interleague deals in 1977 was March 15, so by waiting until after that day to deal Seaver, the Mets lost half their possible trading partners. The team was also locked in a contract dispute with outfielder Dave Kingman, a man who could hit for power but do little else. They'd offered him a six-year, $1.2 million deal, which Kingman refused. Notable here: They were willing to commit almost twice as much money to Dave Kingman as they were to Tom Seaver. Astounding.

Seaver, the loyal union man, spoke out in support of his team-mate. He also criticized M. Donald Grant for calling a team meeting to assert that an exhibition game against the Yankees was a "must-win" contest. Grant's response was not to take the high road.

"He's gone off the deep end," Grant told reporters. "He's disappointed that he didn't get what the free agents got and he can't stand it. He's disappointed that he can't make their money . . . and he didn't have the guts to go for it."

Got that? Seaver was gutless for remaining with the Mets and agreeing to be chronically underpaid. In one fell swoop, Grant managed to ensure that his star pitcher would leave. He publicly exposed how little the Mets thought of Seaver, artificially lowering his trade value. And he put a neon sign in front of Shea Stadium that read: THIS IS HOW WE TREAT OUR PLAYERS. It didn't really matter that it would scare free agents away, of course—the Mets didn't believe in free agency at that time. I can feel the missed opportunities as I write this, the lost Reggie Jacksons, Goose Gossages, and Nolan Ryans. And, naturally, the loss of Seaver most of all.

Finally, the deal came on June 15, 1977. The Mets traded Tom Seaver, the best pitcher in baseball, the man more fans identified as what was great about the New York Mets than all other players combined, to Cincinnati in exchange for four players: Steve Henderson, Pat Zachry, Doug Flynn, and Dan Norman. While the Mets can't be faulted for not knowing the future, ample evidence available at the time shows what a lousy trade this was in the present.

Let's start with Steve Henderson, the most valuable part of the haul. At age twenty-four, Henderson had produced a .901 OPS in a half season of Triple-A after an .888 OPS in a full season of Double-A in 1976. But he was coming to the majors late, which meant growth was unlikely—and his minor-league numbers were likely inflated because he'd been playing with younger guys. And he'd already stagnated defensively as a corner outfielder. In other words, the chances he'd become a star were next to nil. And that's exactly what happened.

It is fair to say that Henderson maxed out his potential as a Met. He posted a 132 OPS+ in his first half season with New York in 1977. But neither power nor speed developed; he hit 23 home runs, total, playing left field from 1978 to 1980, one less than Jim Rice hit in any *one* season during that time. But again, you ask, What did they know at the time of the deal? How about this: As a twenty-three-year-old in 1976, Henderson hit 17 home runs at Double-A. As a twenty-three-year-old in 1976, Rice hit 25 home runs for the Boston Red Sox.

Next on the list was Pat Zachry, the 1976 Rookie of the Year. And Zachry's success in his rookie year at age twenty-four was legit—143 strikeouts, 14 wins, a 2.73 ERA. But a good scout would know it wouldn't last. Zachry had never struck out batters at that clip, and he'd never approached the 204 innings he threw in 1976, either. The season's success was likely an aberration, and who knew what toll all that throwing had taken on him?

Well, actually, the Mets did. Zachry wasn't traded until June, which meant the Mets knew he was 3–7, with an ERA over 5, and that his strikeouts were significantly more rare. All these things should have been warning signs to the Mets. Unsurprisingly, Zachry never again reached his rookie level in innings pitched or strikeout rate. He pitched with the Mets until 1982, struggling through injuries and mediocre performance.

But wait, there's more! Also acquired in the trade: Doug Flynn. The sure-handed second baseman was twenty-six when the Mets acquired him. In other words, the .651 OPS he'd posted thus far wasn't likely to get better—his bat had finished developing. His glove turned out to be as good as advertised, but his bat wasn't even as good as it had been.

I still hear from the odd Mets fan who loves Doug Flynn; in his time, second basemen didn't hit nearly as well as they do today. And they loved his defense. But Flynn's lack of hitting stood out even in his own day. From 1977 to 1981—Flynn's tenure with the Mets—sixteen major leaguers played at least 500 games at second base. Among those sixteen, Flynn's OPS+ of 57 is the lowest, and by a pretty significant margin. Twelve of the sixteen had an OPS+ of at least 82. So it wasn't the era: Doug Flynn was a classically poor bat, regardless of his time. He did win a Gold Glove, though.

But listen. Hindsight is hindsight. The Mets traded one marquee player and got four players in return. Henderson, Zachry, and Flynn were mediocre players, hardly different from the odds and ends the Mets already had lying around. In a blockbuster trade like this one, you looked for guys with real upside, the ones who, five years later, become the centerpiece of the team. The kinds of players you can't imagine *not* having. And in 1977, the Mets general manager knew who that player was.

M. Donald Grant told the media, at the time of the deal, "Twenty years from now, people will remember this as the Dan Norman trade."

Let's all just take a moment to absorb that.

Not even Dan Norman remembers this as the Dan Norman trade. He hit a grand total of 9 home runs in 307 plate appearances as a Met over parts of three seasons. And let's just say he was no Doug Flynn in the outfield. He was two years younger than Steve Henderson but had seen little success in the minors. All it meant was that by the time he was Henderson's age, he had a chance to be as good a prospect as . . . Steve Henderson.

The point is, the Mets weren't unlucky in what history does not remember as the Dan Norman trade. They traded a Hall of Famer, signed to a favorable contract, in the prime of his career. And with unsophisticated scouting, bad timing, and no business savvy, they got back . . . pretty much what you'd expect. A career minor leaguer and three mediocre players with no real potential to get better.

The Mets actually made a similar blunder fifteen years later with David Cone. In this case, the Mets traded a pitcher younger than Seaver—Cone was just twenty-nine—on August 27, 1992, and received two prospects in return: Jeff Kent and Ryan Thompson. In Kent's case, the Mets didn't realize they had a star, and after a few mediocre seasons traded him in a package for Carlos Baerga. In Thompson, the Mets had a center fielder with raw power who struck out way too much. Indeed, in 1,385 career major-league at-bats, Thompson hit 52 home runs and struck out 347 times. Meanwhile, by the time the team contended again in 1997, Cone still rated among the elite pitchers in baseball. If he would have won them just five more games in 1997 and 1998 combined, both teams could have made the playoffs.

So what can we learn from this? Well, the lessons are a bit different in today's marketplace than they were in '77. Seaver required only a three-year contract; indeed, even after continuing to dominate for the Reds in 1977 and 1978, he signed another three-year deal from 1979 to 1981. Cone signed a three-year, $18 million contract the winter after the Mets traded him in 1992. But Cliff Lee and Roy Halladay, to cite two recent examples, show that the best pitchers in baseball today, even at Seaver's age, receive longer-term contracts than that, and at budget-busting prices. Seaver's annual pay from 1979 to 1981? $275,000.

Had the Mets simply chosen to not consistently attack their best player in the press, both through statements from upper management and leaks to the writer Dick Young, they could have retained the best and most popular player in team history for below-market rate. Instead they traded him for four players who meant nothing more to the fans than who they weren't. Jim Rice probably would have been that in the fans' minds too, at least at first. But he'd have been a star the Mets could build around.

Really, the Seaver trade simply typifies the kind of deals the Mets made to help erode the organizational talent of the early seventies into the perennial last-place finishes experienced in Queens by the end of the decade. Ultimately, that's the biggest mistake of all, bigger than not trading Tom Seaver for Jim Rice. The Mets had one of the game's greatest pitchers ever for most of his peak. Instead of competent management leveraging Seaver's best years with other talented players, the Mets lay siege to their own organization and ruined it, top to bottom. The trade is known as the "Midnight Massacre," due to the timing of it late on the night of June 15. But the truth is, by the time Seaver was packing his bags, the Mets were already dead.

And I had visions of the team doing the same thing with the peaks of Jose Reyes and David Wright, the two players I'd imagined would be my generation's Tom Seaver but with a happier ending. I couldn't go back in time and change the Tom Seaver story, *Quantum Leap*–style. But I had the chance—in fact, the obligation—to change the story for Wright, Reyes, and the next generation of the potentially devastated.

Chapter 9

A GM GROWS IN BROOKLYN

R ACHEL AND I have been partial-season ticket holders
for quite some time now. Naturally, we don't go back
nearly as far as some of the loyal fans, people who came to Shea
Stadium since it opened in 1964 and have continued at Citi
Field. But I'm not sure anyone appreciates being in a glorious
building filled with Mets fans more than I do. See, I grew up
in Phillies country.

That meant my first game, which my father can date to
about 1983 or 1984, took place at Veterans Stadium. Now—
and I say this without any malice for Phillies fans—Veterans
Stadium was not a great place for baseball. The seats were remote, the field was made of artificial turf (and not the good
stuff; one can only speculate as to how many knees met their
demise on that concrete), and the stands were filled with people who cared more about the Eagles. Still, I loved the chance
to get to Veterans Stadium and see the Mets play every time
they came to town, usually twice per series.

But for whatever reason, we never made it to Shea Stadium
while I was a child. We'd take trips to New York, but they'd

usually revolve around theater and museums. Maybe it was simply that we could see the Mets in Philadelphia; we couldn't see Broadway shows in Philadelphia, or get food from Ratner's or Sammy's. Regardless, I attended more than a hundred baseball games as a child; I saw the Mets (and others) countless times at the Vet, watched them battle the Expos in Montreal. I saw future Mets playing in Single-A Pittsfield. I saw former Mets when we'd travel to see the Atlantic City Surf.

And though many Mets fans may have taken it for granted, for me Shea Stadium was a beacon: I knew I had to get there, no matter what it took. I arrived at Bard College for my freshman year in mid-August 1998, and on September 6, I took the Metro-North train down to Manhattan and the 7 train to Shea Stadium.

I'd like to tell you that the Mets rewarded my nearly two decades of loyal support in exile with a truly spectacular show. I'd like to tell you that Mike Piazza hit two home runs, then pointed to me in the stands so I'd know that he knew I'd been listening through the static all along. That John Franco, whom I'd rooted for since 1989—before my voice changed—came on for the save, and I got to see the Atlanta Braves, heads down, disappear into the clubhouse, defeated. But it was not to be.

September 6 was a Saturday-afternoon game, starting just twelve hours after the contest ended the night before. Mike Piazza didn't even play. Instead, my Shea debut, the game I'd dreamed of seeing for all of my conscious life, was caught by . . . Jorge Fabregas. Nothing against Jorge, but it wasn't the same. Braves ace John Smoltz, however, was as dominating live as he'd been on the radio and, occasionally, television. He pitched a complete-game three-hit shutout, struck out 12, didn't walk anyone. Rick Reed, a personal favorite, pitched well into the eighth but simply couldn't measure up to Smoltz. It was, in a way, an appropriate first experience: a microcosm of the entire Atlanta–New York rivalry over roughly the past twenty years.

But I wasn't upset. There were too many reasons to celebrate the day. To walk off the 7 train and down the stairs I'd seen since I was little on the Channel 9 WWOR broadcasts was a thrill itself. In front of the stadium painted blue and orange—not the nondescript concrete of Veterans Stadium, but Mets colors—people sold hats, shirts, teddy bears, all of them decorated to support the Mets. The fans wore the shirts of Piazza, Alfonzo, and Olerud, with more than a smattering of Hernandez, Strawberry, even Agee and Seaver thrown in. When the Mets did well, they cheered. When the opposing team did well, they didn't. To a hometown fan, this sounds obvious. But until you've had the opposite experience, until you've sat in a hard plastic chair with your head in your hands during a low moment and watched forty thousand people cheering—cheering!—at your misfortune, you do not know what luck you've had.

I was rooting for the home team. This was spectacular.

I returned to Shea several more times in 1999, while my father and I made it to Philly to see the Mets come back from down 6–0 to beat the Phillies, 9–7. But as September rolled around and it appeared that the Mets would finally make the playoffs, I knew that nothing would keep me from going to Shea with my dad for a playoff game. It had been eleven years since the Mets even made the playoffs, and who knew when it would happen again?

The playoff tickets went on sale on a Saturday morning, nine A.M., late September. The Mets were in the process of taking two of three from the Phillies to close to within a game of the Braves. The National League's best record was in sight; the

Mets had a three-game lead in the wild-card standings, should they fail to catch Atlanta. I decided to dream big. I dialed and redialed the Mets ticket office. I dialed with abandon, as I'd never dialed before. And like all men of strong will, I made my desires a reality: two tickets, very high in the right-field seats, for the second game of the NLCS. If the Mets were the higher seed, it would be Game 2; if the lower seed, Game 4. They were a birthday gift for my father. If I didn't take action, he might never see a home playoff game, and I couldn't let that happen.

But I was punished for my hubris. The Mets left town for Atlanta and promptly lost seven in a row. The following weekend, my father and I watched them drop games five and six of the streak at Veterans Stadium, where an utterly forgettable Phillies team went on to sweep them. The Phils ran out a starting pitcher named Joe Grahe, who had such unimpressive stuff that my father predicted, correctly, that he'd be out of the league by the end of the year. He pitched eight innings to this desperate Mets team, allowing only a single earned run.

He wouldn't pitch another full inning for the rest of his major-league career, but he was too much for my team.

I returned to campus swamped with work, including a big, intimidating paper, the longest I had ever been assigned. I decided to knock out all my other work for the week, saving the paper for the weekend. And as the Mets proceeded to lose two more to Atlanta, dropping two games behind Cincinnati for the wild card (while the Braves had clinched a while back), it appeared I'd have nothing but time to work on the paper ahead of Wednesday morning's class. My team's playoff hopes rested on a series of unlikely contingencies, and after watching them fritter away the advantages they had, I was more content to turn away.

But, of course, this is the Mets. That unlikely scenario is exactly what happened. The Mets, who had been losing one-run games, beat the Pirates by a single run in eleven innings on Friday, routed them on Saturday, and won on Sunday, 2–1, on a game-ending wild pitch. Hardly the stuff of dynasties, but they got the job done. Meanwhile, Cincinnati lost Friday, lost Saturday, and only by winning a rain-delayed game late Sunday evening did they manage to force a one-game playoff for the wild card Monday night.

I didn't get any work done on the paper that weekend. Can you blame me? I was an obsessive baseball fan with unlimited access to a new invention that made my obsessions that much easier to indulge: the Internet. It didn't matter if you were an important term paper, a cabinet of high-end liquor, or a busful of friendly coeds. This was a pennant race, and if you weren't baseball, I wasn't interested.

And right now the whole baseball world was watching. Even though the Mets should have locked up their playoff spot easily, they were now bracing for an opportunity to do it in the most dramatic way possible. No term paper, regardless of the due date, was going to stand between me and baseball history.

The Reds were a gritty, slugging team in the midst of an improbable run. They weren't flashy, but with steady contributions from Greg Vaughn, Sean Casey, Mike Cameron, and Dmitri Young, they were one of those top-to-bottom teams you couldn't relax against. They had already won 96 games, the most they'd managed since the 1970s, and looked as if they were on a mission.

But that Mets team, frankly, was even better. This was the Mets of Mike Piazza (40 homers, .936 OPS) in his prime; of Robin Ventura and Edgardo Alfonzo's career years; and of one

Alois Terry Leiter. On the final day of the season in 1999, as I jealously guarded the Bard student center's only TV, keeping out the *Buffy the Vampire Slayer* fans, Al Leiter was all I needed.

Leiter was thirty-three years young and had been sloppy through most of September, including two clunkers at the exact wrong time, in the midst of the Mets' late-season losing streak. But on October 4 he was masterful. Nine shutout innings, two hits, and a bottle of champagne, sprayed liberally, to celebrate. That Leiter would go on to experience a rare type of late-career surge, winning 70 more games as a big-league starter, was all just icing on the cake. The important thing was we were in and the Reds were out.

The tickets hadn't been a curse. The Mets were going to the playoffs. They'd be playing in Arizona, Tuesday night at eleven. That paper was due at ten Wednesday morning. But the Mets were about to play their first postseason game since I was eight. Everything else would have to wait.

Back in the student center, I was joined by many of the same Mets fans from the night before: We became a close-knit group during those playoffs. And what followed was a truly entertaining game. Against Randy Johnson, a pitcher I found it easy to root against due to his demeanor, the Mets scored early. Arizona spotted them a 4–0 lead but came back against Masato Yoshii and tied the game in the sixth. Despite giving up early runs, Johnson pitched into the ninth. But he ran out of gas there, with Robin Ventura and Rey Ordonez hitting singles; Melvin Mora then walked. On came hard-throwing Bobby Chouinard. He got Rickey Henderson for the second out. But Edgardo Alfonzo, one of the best players in Mets history, hit his second home run of the game, a grand slam, to provide the margin of victory. Armando Benitez recorded the save at 2:02 A.M. I ran home—too energized to walk, despite having eaten nothing but Combos—and called my father to talk about the game.

I wrote the paper instead of going to sleep—who could sleep anyway after a game like that? It was possibly the easiest assignment I'd ever done. For every obscure page citation I looked up, some primordial part of me was doing it for Edgardo Alfonzo. Or better yet, I was doing it to be one step closer to a playoff game that I could attend with my father. I finished at six thirty that morning and got an A.

It was one of my finest memories of college, and I have no shortage of them. More on the playoff game with my father to come.

A few years later I met Rachel, and we moved to Rockland County in 2006. Suddenly, Shea Stadium was an easy drive— forty-five minutes without traffic. And as that 2006 season continued and we attended more and more games, I realized that buying a partial-season plan would guarantee us playoff tickets. Never mind scalpers or the long odds of the redial button— we'd have the chance to see the playoffs ourselves. After several days of convincing, my father agreed as well. He was normally reluctant to do anything impulsive, but the memories we had of 1999 and 2000 were simply too good to ignore.

Naturally, our seats weren't great—way up the first base line, Section 25 of the loge, beginning with the September 8 game against the Dodgers. And while the Mets lost, 5–0, we looked at it less as a disappointing loss—after all, the team still had a fifteen-and-a-half-game lead—and more like a down payment for games still to come.

But while future postseasons seemed to beckon after that first year, actual postseasons didn't. I didn't regret renewing my season tickets each year. But that's not to say the Mets didn't try and make me.

Unlike every other team in baseball, the Mets offered no discount for partial- or season-plan holders. In other words, you give the Mets all your money up front, and they'll . . . take your money. For many years, the only appreciation the Mets showed plan and season-ticket holders was a gift and media guide. And even that got progressively more limited. One off-season, the gift was an artist's rendering of a shovel mounted on a ceramic tile. It commemorated the groundbreaking of the new stadium, which was nice, but it was also . . . stupid. What was I going to do with a tile? Another year, the gift failed to come at all. And this past year, a gift arrived that—well, I don't quite know how to describe it.

The package was kind of a lamp-shaped contraption that, if you plugged it in, would keep a plastic Mets baseball suspended in midair—a little like that parlor trick with a Ping-Pong ball and a hair dryer. But it didn't work. Still, long after I put it out with the weekly recycle, I kept wondering: Why would I possibly want a contraption that kept a plastic Mets baseball suspended in midair? As Caryn Rose, the creator of Metsgrrl.com and host of my upcoming primary wrote, "The fact that this has to be plugged in to work completely negates any carbon offsets the Mets received from not sending out printed media guides."

One supposes this was a makeup for the holiday picture, a framed photo of Citi Field that went out with the following note: "Thank you for your support of the Mets in 2009. The enclosed photo commemorates our Inaugural Opening Day at Citi Field. On behalf of everyone at the Mets, best wishes for a happy holiday season and new year." Sounds nice, right? Only problem was, I received it on February 2. One assumes the holiday season the Mets were referring to was Groundhog Day, and the new year was Chinese.

These are petty complaints, I know. In truth, I really don't care if the Mets don't want to send out catalogs, or tiles, or lamplike baseball-suspension devices. What I really want is to get back that feeling of connection I had as a college freshman, making my first trip to Shea. And these plastic oddities are meant to be a gesture, or a message to fans that we matter. I think sending a months-late holiday photo to season ticket holders sends a different message: "You are an afterthought." And when combined with a complete lack of other communication, you've created a customer problem. Sure enough, people simply weren't showing up in 2010, even before the Mets fell out of the pennant race.

I knew this would be a problem months earlier when I tried, to the seeming shock of the hardworking people in the ticket office, to upgrade my seats for 2010. The upgrade got delayed several weeks, then several months, as the Mets tried to convince former plan holders to return to the fold. Once that effort ended, the ticket department explained that all the former season and plan holders needed to be cleared from the system before ticket requests could be considered. I said during one conversation, "It sure seems to be taking a long time. Do you have more than usual?"

"You have no idea," a seemingly weary rep responded.

Eventually, I moved to the section I desired for much of the winter. It felt like a mixed blessing. It wasn't so long ago that I had been attacking the redial button, just hoping to pry open Shea Stadium enough to get inside for a playoff game. I had felt like part of something. Sitting in a mostly empty Section 508, it felt more like . . . I was one of the suckers who didn't get it.

It was unnerving, particularly as I plotted to introduce my daughter to the very same set of emotions.

As the Megdal for GM campaign continued, I pushed forward in my attempts to speak to, and receive the blessing from, two disparate sets of Mets fans. My Metsgrrl.com primary, I felt, was a referendum on my ability to speak to the concerns I shared with other fans about how the Mets handled their ticket sales. And over at MetsMinorLeagueBlog.com, Toby Hyde hosted a primary among Mets fans mainly obsessed with the team's organizational performance.

I'd known Toby since he started an e-mail Listserv about the Mets' minor-league system back in the early part of the decade. According to Toby, I was one of the first fifteen or twenty people to whom he sent a diligent daily look at all Mets prospects, from Triple-A to the Gulf Coast League. But we'd both progressed significantly since then. Toby now worked as the voice of the Savannah Sand Gnats, a Class-A affiliate of the New York Mets, and wrote about the system for the SNY-affiliated Mets Minor League Blog. Still, he accepted my offer to become my minor-league director without hesitation.

Fortunately, a pair of items vital to both the New York Mets and my view of them had popped up—one that spoke directly to the way the Mets treated potential customers, the other to just how prospects were developed within the system.

In late June, perhaps inspired by the lack of turnout at Citi Field, the Mets began an ad campaign urging people to purchase tickets "Directly from the Mets." Left unsaid was that many people, rather than going to Mets.com or calling the ubiquitous 718-507-TIXX number I'd memorized since childhood from the radio broadcasts, were simply buying tickets from

Stubhub.com instead. The reasons were clear, as I explained on MegdalforGM.com.

If you've been watching Mets games regularly lately, you've been bombarded by a commercial that urges you to buy Mets tickets "directly from the source," touting "better seats" and "lower prices." It certainly seems fair to infer from this new campaign that many fans are skipping the Mets entirely and simply buying tickets from the resale market.

While some may say that is exactly what the Mets and other MLB teams deserve for turning Stubhub.com from competitor into licensed scalper, that obscures the larger problem here: The only reason Mets fans choose Stubhub over Mets.com is the ability to choose where to sit!

Ask a baseball fan about attending a baseball game, and the answer will usually include a place in the ballpark he or she likes to sit. For me, that is between home plate and first base. Others prefer between home and third, or a specific section, or out in the outfield, etc.

Now, go to Mets.com and try to get tickets to a particular game in that area. No luck, right? Because on Mets.com, your only choice is to pick a price level.

Nobody says, "I enjoy watching a baseball game from $64 seats."

When I am elected the next general manager of the Mets, a complete overhaul of the way fans are able to buy tickets will take place immediately. This is best for the fans, who can buy tickets without a markup, and best for the Mets, who will sell many more of their own tickets.

And to be sure, when someone suggests taking up valuable

advertising time during Mets games trying to convince fans not to pay a premium no one wants to pay for tickets, I'll make a simple suggestion:

Let's make buying tickets a less frustrating experience for fans. LOGIC means that it is time for the 2010 Mets to sell tickets using 2010 technology.

I heard from a lot of fans about that piece. And it made sense that I would. The technology existed. The Mets just didn't use it. Instead of attacking the problem by making it easier to buy tickets from them, they put out an ad campaign telling people it was easier. Not surprisingly, this didn't work.

Of course, this didn't stop me from wanting to attend Citi Field. Really, nothing would. The writer Greg Prince of Faith and Fear in Flushing has written about getting the distinct impression that the Mets viewed their fans as an inconvenience rather than their lifeblood. I knew precisely the feeling. I'd decided to attend a game, last-minute, back in September 2003. The Mets were well on their way to a 66–95 record, and getting tickets proved very easy, day of game, at the ticket window. Being a poor young journalist, I purchased the least expensive tickets, in the upper reserved section.

Somewhere in the vicinity of the seventh inning, with the Mets trailing the Marlins, 4–3, I tried to move down from my empty upper reserved section to the upper box. At Shea Stadium, this was always accomplished with a large helping of fear—the staff seemed trained to make you feel as terrible as possible about wanting a closer look at a baseball game. Naturally, an usher quickly came over, began yelling at me for moving down, and threatened to have me ejected from the stadium. He was within his rights to do this, I suppose. But it is fair to wonder what the Mets gain from such behavior.

"It's the seventh inning!" I protested. I motioned to the empty upper box section. "There's no one here!" I motioned to the upper reserved section I'd just vacated. "There's no one there! What is the problem?"

"The problem is you didn't buy that ticket!" the man replied. "Either get back where you belong or you're gone."

I looked out at a sea of red seats. The posted attendance for this game, I later learned, was 16,669—roughly a quarter of the stadium's capacity. It was a cloudy Wednesday afternoon. The Mets were twenty games under .500 and they'd lost six in a row. The Mets had rolled out mostly minor leaguers and scrubs—the kinds of players only the real diehards would come out to see. And suddenly I couldn't take it anymore.

"I'm the only one who still wants to see this team! I drove an hour and a half to do it! But look around. I'm it!"

The usher was unmoved and repeated his vow to have me thrown out of the stadium. I wanted to leave, but I wanted baseball more. I returned to my original seat. I couldn't walk away from my team.

Like I said, it often felt lonely rooting for the Mets. And I'd heard too many stories like this one to believe I'd experienced an isolated incident. But it did make something I experienced at Citizens Bank Park in Philadelphia seem like an optical illusion.

On July 4, 2008, Rachel and I took the train down to Philly to see Johan Santana and the Mets take on the Phillies. We'd purchased tickets last-minute, making sure to get the best available tickets that were also under cover, given the threat of rain.

We'd found seats in the section directly behind home plate, about twenty rows back. The view was absolutely perfect. And with intermittent rain, we were happy for the shelter. Even surrounded by Phillies fans, Citizens Bank Park is a lovely place to watch a baseball game.

In the seventh inning of a tense 2–2 game, we saw a group of four teenagers make their way down to the third row from the field, sitting in empty seats. Shortly thereafter, an usher followed, and we'd been to Shea too many times to doubt what would happen next—an accusation, a defeated group moved from otherwise-unused seats, an unhappy memory created at the ballpark.

Instead, the usher proceeded to ask the kids if he could dry the seats for them. He did so not because he had any reason to expect a tip or because he thought they had purchased the seats. The Phillies had trained their employees, clearly, to treat fans with respect. The kids didn't cause problems; they just watched their favorite team up close on a rainy night for a few innings. I'm willing to bet it made them more excited to come back to the ballpark, too. I bet they bought more tickets.

There was something utterly soul-crushing about being treated so nicely every time I attended a Phillies game. It was beastly, just on a personal level, to be so accommodated by a team I'd been taught to revile. I had no idea how to respond to that. But more than that, it also served as a reminder that just up the New Jersey Turnpike, things could be done differently, too. And as my online primaries continued, I prayed that I could change them myself.

Over at Metsgrrl.com, things were going well. My screed against the Amazin' Mets' ticket practices had gone over well, and many sympathetic votes were cast. But Toby's site was a tougher nut to crack. I was seeing real opposition, and I couldn't help wondering whether I could do more to burnish my credentials.

A few weeks before, I'd convinced an editor to let me take an evening in Coney Island, evaluating Mets prospect Cory Vaughn of the Brooklyn Cyclones. The team had spent a fourth-round pick on him in 2010. Not only did I think this would make a great story, but I was challenging myself as a future GM to evaluate him as a prospect in person.

Perspectives were clearly mixed on Vaughn, a six-foot-three, 225-pound outfielder. He came with a big-league pedigree, as the son of slugger Greg Vaughn, and he'd played for Hall of Famer Tony Gwynn in college at San Diego State. But ESPN .com's Keith Law saw him play once in college and came to the conclusion that any team to draft Vaughn would have a lemon on their hands. As he wrote in February, before the Mets drafted him: "San Diego State's Cory Vaughn is an athletic outfielder who looks good in the uniform and has good bloodlines (he's Greg Vaughn's son), all of which will probably lead to his being overdrafted in June despite how unrefined he is as a hitter . . . His bigger problem, however, is horrible plate discipline: He swings at everything and doesn't make enough contact." Later, after the Mets drafted him, Law would see Vaughn play with the Cyclones. His opinion did not change.

Law had spent time in the Toronto Blue Jays' front office before going to work for ESPN, so he'd been on both sides of player evaluation. Would I come to the same conclusion? I'd take the time to evaluate Vaughn as I would if I were the GM: I'd look at his stats, I'd see him play, I'd talk to him. Arguably, as GM I wouldn't have the luxury of even this much time on a single player—such things would be delegated. But without those skills, I wouldn't know exactly what to look for in the reports of my subordinates, either.

It was unseasonably hot, which is saying something for July, as I waited for Vaughn in the Brooklyn dugout around an hour before game time. Meanwhile, the Cyclones were honoring Angel Pagan, a 2001 Brooklyn Cyclone made good, with a retired number. I watched Pagan soak up the adulation of the crowd and reflected on what it was that allowed him to become one of the most valuable members of the 2010 Mets. In our conversations he was thoughtful, and discussed his tireless work ethic and his physical talent. Could I have predicted stardom for Pagan way back in 2001?

Vaughn walked down the clubhouse tunnel and joined me in the dugout. I'd been interviewing professional baseball players around and on the field for years; it still provided a thrill. We began to talk baseball, and his studying of the game was obvious—he wasn't relying on a big swing and hope, the way he'd been portrayed by Law. Indeed, Law had said his swing would keep him from maximizing "his power potential," but Vaughn had hit long home runs in bunches since debuting as a pro. And while he struck out 55 times in 188 at-bats in his senior year at SDSU, he'd struck out just 27 times in his first 142 at-bats with Brooklyn.

The more we spoke, the more impressive Vaughn became. He'd dealt with diabetes since childhood and had expressed in other interviews his desire to help children who suffered as well. But it wasn't an idle thought—Vaughn knew exactly how he'd go about becoming a children's endocrinologist and had taken many of the premed courses at SDSU in case baseball didn't work out. Each of his responses seemed to indicate a longer-range thinker.

"One of the biggest things for me has been not to let a bad first at-bat, second at-bat ruin the rest of my game," Vaughn said. "In college, I'd let a bad start affect my concentration the rest of the way. Preparing so that I'm mentally prepared for the entire game has been key."

That night, Vaughn went hitless. But he went deep into each at-bat, and the results included a screaming liner right at the left fielder. Playing right field, he handled several chances flawlessly, displayed an impressive throwing arm, and gave every indication that his tools were well on their way to becoming skills. I decided to let Cory Vaughn be a measuring stick for myself. I believed that Keith Law had him wrong. And I was excited to see whether my take on Vaughn would win the day.

I knew even before I'd started the piece that my writing had clearly not focused enough on the minor leagues in general. Thanks to my consistent writing in support of Mets ticket holders, I'd won an overwhelming mandate at Metsgrrl.com, capturing more than 73 percent of the vote. But I survived a close scare at Toby Hyde's blog, winning narrowly, with 53 percent. Clearly, I'd need to do more to burnish my minor-league credentials in the coming weeks. Fortunately for my campaign, and unfortunately for the future of the Mets, Jenrry Mejia loomed as a case study in exactly how not to treat a prospect.

Chapter 10

TO SEEK A NEWER WORLD

THERE ARE NO guarantees when it comes to developing baseball prospects. Signing players ranging in age from sixteen to about twenty-one, making judgments about their baseball potential with little statistical information and no ability to know how bodies will change, not to mention the many unknowable factors inherent in the future—it is nearly impossible to project an individual's impact on a major-league team at the time he is drafted.

But still—you have to draft them. As the future GM of the team, I knew I had to take responsibility for maximizing the potential of the prospects in the Mets organization. And the knowledge that prospect development is so time-consuming and uncertain should in itself drive the decision-making process in each case. Unfortunately, the Mets have failed to follow these basic guidelines again and again.

Jenrry Mejia provides a window into several of these practices, along with something the team does right: activity in international markets. Mejia signed in April 2007 out of the Dominican Republic. Players outside the United States and

Canada are not subject to the rules of baseball's amateur draft. They are free to sign with the highest bidder. In an example of good scouting, the Mets managed to snag Mejia for just $16,500. They sent him to the Dominican Summer League in 2007, then saw him split time in 2008 between the Gulf Coast League and the Brooklyn Cyclones—the low end of the minor leagues. He excelled at each stop. So far, so good.

In 2009, Mejia began the year with the Class-A St. Lucie Mets, three levels away from the major leagues. In 50⅓ innings, his ERA was 1.97 over nine starts. Despite a lack of refinement with his secondary pitches, he was overpowering Class-A hitters with his fastball. The Mets chose to promote him to Double-A Binghamton, which isn't indefensible but does speak to an organization-wide tendency to promote quickly instead of allowing a player to hone his skills. Since Mejia was still just nineteen years old, I'd have let him finish the year at Single-A while throwing more of his secondary pitches—the skill that would determine whether he could succeed in the major leagues or not. That's the whole point of the system, after all.

When Mejia got to Double-A, he found his fastball wasn't enough. His ERA ballooned to 4.47 over 10 starts and he missed some time due to injury. Now, his long-term prospects were still very solid—he struck out 9.5 batters per nine innings, for instance, a very strong positive indicator of future success—but his walk rate was an unsightly 4.7 per nine, and the results made it clear that he was far from a finished product. The clear answer: another season of Double-A, greater emphasis on secondary pitches, letting him continue to learn how to pitch. Remember: This was a nineteen-year-old kid with about 200 professional innings, total, in his career.

What the Mets did instead was bring Mejia to spring training, let their field manager see him in relief, then choose him for the major-league roster. There are so many problems with this, it is hard to know where to start. For one thing, Mejia's ability to succeed as a major-league starter—something incredibly valuable—would be dictated by his ability to throw large quantities of innings and master his secondary pitches. (I'm not making these rules up, by the way. Any baseball person would say the same thing. Ask Peter Gammons. He never lies.)

Pitching in a major-league bullpen would allow him to accomplish exactly none of those things. He'd get short stints, irregularly spaced, and a premium would be placed on him throwing his fastball. The longer he spent in the bullpen, the lower his innings total would be for 2010, making it that much harder to groom him to throw 200 innings in 2011 and beyond. And because he had never pitched out of the bullpen before, it was unknown whether the change in schedule would lead to an injury.

So why did they do it? In short, to win games at the major-league level. Not such an ignoble goal, of course. But it was fundamentally shortsighted, and, as a fan, that drove me nuts.

Unfortunately, the Mets then took this situation and made it more infuriating. If the decision had been made to move Mejia to the bullpen in 2010, at least that was a plan. I objected to it, but you could make the case, at least, that he could still learn on the job in that role. Mejia could train to become a reliever, less valuable than a starter but still a useful player. But that's not what happened. Instead the Mets engaged in what Jerry Manuel later referred to as "a daily debate" over how to deploy Mejia. He pitched irregularly. Sometimes Mejia would pitch four times in six days; other times, three times in two weeks. Manuel had pushed for Mejia, claiming he needed him in the bullpen. But once he got him, Manuel used him as a spare part.

After nearly three months of this, the Mets finally sent Mejia to the minor leagues at the end of June. The future, it seemed, had won the day: He could develop as a player, learn his pitches, and come back as the starter I dreamed he could be. But this too was mishandled. Rather than stretch him out in the customary manner, they pitched Mejia for 60 pitches, on three days of rest, three consecutive times. Predictably, he came down with a shoulder injury, and less than two months later that same pitching shoulder ended his season. Like I said: a debacle in every way.

This may sound like technical complaining—in fact, it is. But if I didn't have technical complaints about the way the organization was run, what business did I have campaigning to run it? Besides, failing to handle Jenrry Mejia right did something else: It spoiled what should be a joyous experience for fans. The debut of a young, talented graduate of the farm system is supposed to be a wonderful experience, filled with hope and excitement. This is what I wanted for little Mirabelle, my own top-flight prospect of a different kind.

David Wright is a perfect example of how to properly handle a prospect. Drafted as a sandwich pick (between the first and second rounds) in 2001, he began his career in rookie-league Kingsport and posted a .300/.391/.458 season line. Promoted to Capital City, rather than St. Lucie—a lower-pressure A-ball— Wright continued to excel, hitting .266/.367/.401. Again, he was given a full season. The next season, he hit .270/.369/.459 for St. Lucie, earning a promotion to Double-A Binghamton in 2004. Only once he absolutely murdered Double-A pitching—.363/.467/.619—and did the same thing at Triple-A did he get the call from the Mets. And once with the Mets, he was the everyday third baseman, allowing his development to continue. It's no surprise, then, that Wright has been the most successful Met of the decade, or that his success at the major-league level began immediately.

And it should come as no surprise, either, that nearly every other Mets prospect has been unnecessarily rushed, with disappointing results. Jose Reyes had an OPS of just .690 at Triple-A when the Mets promoted him in 2003. Unsurprisingly, he posted an OPS of just .698 from 2003 to 2005, even with his physical gifts. Reyes finally figured it out by 2006, but not before the Mets wasted his three least-expensive seasons. In the case of Reyes, they didn't ruin a prospect, they just made him unnecessarily expensive.

Other rushed prospects have not been so lucky. Carlos Gomez came through the minor-league system with the gift of incredible speed, greater than that of Reyes. Which is wonderful—as long as you get on base. Gomez was promoted to Double-A at the tender age of twenty and made his Mets debut before turning twenty-two. At no point did he display the slightest bit of patience at the plate. And in four major-league seasons since, his OPS has been a putrid .642. Would remaining in the minors have taught him to recognize pitches? Impossible to know. But the Mets never allowed themselves, or Gomez, to find out. He was traded to Minnesota less than a year after being brought to the majors.

Learning to play baseball at any level can be a grinding, pressure-filled experience. It may seem academic whether a player learns to hit sliders thrown by college-age minor leaguers or Randy Johnson, but it's not. You can't skip your students up two grades just because they ace their math classes. When I'm

GM, there will be no favoritism and no social promotions. You've got to earn your way up.

Consider Mike Pelfrey, the team's top pick in 2005. After just 96 minor-league innings, Pelfrey made his major-league debut in 2006. He returned to Triple-A in 2007, but ultimately pitched less than 180 minor-league innings total before the Mets asked him to assume a regular spot in the rotation. It took four years of major-league futility before he showed signs of maturity, consistently deploying secondary pitches to match his dominating fastball. In the meantime he's had to listen to the media debate whether he was a bust, gained three years toward becoming an expensive free agent, and lost several high-pressure games in the pennant races of 2007 and 2008. What was gained by this? And who knows how much better off he'd be if he'd had actual minor-league growth?

Just for comparison, Clay Buchholz was drafted by the Boston Red Sox in 2005. And he was, relative to Boston prospects, hurried through the system—mainly because he put up ridiculous numbers at practically every stop. He logged well over 440 innings in the minor leagues before taking a regular rotation spot with Boston in 2010, becoming arguably the team's best pitcher. Rare is the pitcher who should be rushed like Pelfrey—Tim Lincecum logged just $62\frac{2}{3}$ minor-league innings because he was striking out 14.9 hitters per nine innings and had an ERA of 1.01. And you know right away whether it's a good plan—Lincecum has already won two Cy Young awards and a World Series. Put it this way: When a pitcher's nickname is the Freak, that's probably a sign he shouldn't be your organization's template.

But the Mets rushed Pelfrey, Gomez, even Reyes because they simply didn't have the talent in their farm system to allow the good prospects a chance to properly ripen. (In better organizations, the Double- and Triple-A squads are well stocked with players who can substitute if the major-league team suffers injuries, allowing the young talent to continue developing behind them.) And here, again, the Mets created their own problem. Each year Major League Baseball publishes guidelines that recommend how much bonus money teams should pay to each draft pick: a certain amount for number one, a little less for number two, and so on. It's known informally as that pick's "slot." However, teams can, if they choose, go "over slot" on a particular draft pick. And a few teams do—as Baseball Prospectus's Kevin Goldstein put it, "smart ones and rich ones."

Well, except the Mets. They're rich, but they've consistently failed to go over slot, even as the Yankees, Red Sox, Phillies, and some other teams use this loophole to nab prospects. Yes, it's economic bullying, but the rules of baseball allow it. And it's no worse, ethically speaking, than overpaying for a major-league free agent, something the Mets do almost as policy. Here's how it works: Any number of players who believe they are talented enough to earn a large bonus, but perhaps not good enough to be taken in the top five or ten overall picks, will let it be known through their agents that they require more money to sign than their likely slot. Wealthier teams then have the chance to draft these players late in the first round, or even in later rounds, because the teams who don't want to spend over slot won't pick them. The net result is that teams like the Red Sox and Yankees procure much more talent from each draft than the Mets do.

Frankly, you don't even need to be rich to draft over slot. The Kansas City Royals and Pittsburgh Pirates, hardly baseball's high rollers, have allocated additional money to the draft and international signings in recent seasons. Their systems have begun to reap the benefits. Look at it this way: The average major leaguer makes well over $3 million per season, but for their first three years, nearly every young player makes the major-league minimum of $400,000. Even a midlevel player developed through the system can provide similar or better production for a fraction of a veteran; and the team controls that player's rights for six full seasons, usually during that player's peak age. This is why it was so foolish to bring Jose Reyes up in 2003, when he had a meager OPS of .698 and the Mets won exactly nothing. Three years later he was a big-league prodigy, an All-Star at age twenty-four, and helped take the Mets to the NLCS—yet they were already paying him $3 million per year. He'll make $11 million next year.

Instead of progressing in this way, the Mets managed to take several steps back in international spending to complement their draft budgets. In the amateur draft from 2008 to 2010, their bonus spending ranked twenty-sixth. "The bottom line," said Jim Callis, *Baseball America*'s executive editor, "is they just have not spent on the draft, and they have not spent internationally." Put another, more upsetting way: The Mets spent less on the draft in 2008, 2009, or 2010 than they spent on the combined salaries of Alex Cora, Gary Matthews Jr., and Mike Jacobs. Put an even more upsetting way, they spent less on the draft in any of those years than they spent on the salary of just Jeff Francoeur. Put in the most upsetting way of all, they spent less on the draft from 2008 to 2010, combined, than they did on the single-season salaries of Luis Castillo and Oliver Perez in each of the last two seasons.

In the scheme of major-league salaries, spending well on the draft isn't very expensive—$11 to $12 million. It's less per year than the Mets spent on Jason Bay. And in the end it actually saves money, because the price of the big-league roster goes down. Not to mention making every team at every level of your organization better.

Naturally, these two problems—rushing prospects and not enough prospects—reinforced one another. Without enough prospects to go around, and the major-league team needing help, the temptation to push the talented kid in A-ball a little sooner proved overwhelming. And when rushing proved to be an inapt way to produce young talent, the natural response was to draft low-ceiling, relatively complete college pitchers— the kind that came cheap. A great example of this was Eddie Kunz, whom the Mets drafted with the forty-second overall pick in 2007, then rushed through mediocre minor-league performances and into the majors by 2008—where he failed. The year before, drafting in nearly the same exact spot, the Yankees went over slot and landed Joba Chamberlain, who promptly struck out nearly 14 batters per nine innings en route to the major leagues.

It was impossible not to envy Yankees fans when Joba made his debut. A huge Nebraska farm boy who threw ninety-nine miles per hour, with secondary pitches that differed greatly in both speed and movement from that fastball, the Yankees certainly didn't bring him to the major leagues before he had the skills to succeed there. And as a result, they experienced the thrill of a prospect debut. (I blame his subsequent struggles on Yankee impatience.)

Earlier, I spoke about the Mets' propensity to buy late-career free agents whose value is akin to that of a used car. Well, for a fan, seeing a top prospect make his debut is akin to that spectacular feeling of buying a brand-new car and driving it off the lot. Everything the rookie does—the first hit, the first home run, the first diving catch—is infused with excitement (and also new-car smell). Fans follow the minor leagues like never before, catching video clips and scouting reports the way a prospective car buyer checks out *Car and Driver* or the Kelley Blue Book. And finally, after years of anticipation, the moment arrives. That new car belongs to us.

In other words: Not only is a burgeoning farm system capable of providing players with the most value in baseball, both for the roster itself and as chips in trade, but those players are easily the most capable of inspiring loyalty from the fan base.

So the way the Mets stocked and ran their farm system was going to have to change. And thanks to one of my delegates, I'd have the chance to tell scores of Mets fans just that—with one of my professional heroes listening in as well. My first campaign appearance promised to be a good one.

Chapter 11

THE ARC OF HISTORY IS LONG,
BUT IT BENDS TOWARD JUSTICE

W HEN GREG PRINCE, Mets blogger nonpareil and potential delegate over at Faith and Fear in Flushing, invited me to give my stump speech at the periodic Mets fan
meet-up he hosts, I immediately knew that this was precisely
the opportunity I craved.

The scene was ideal: At Two Boots Grand Central Pizzeria,
Mets fans by the score would be ready to hear my message.
The owner, Phil Hartman, saw to that by instituting an un-
usual price for each beer: one Mets baseball card. Finally I'd
have the chance to test my ideas in front of a live audience!

I also knew I would be merely an undercard. Marty Noble,
the longtime baseball writer, was also coming to share stories
from his forty-plus years writing about the game with *Newsday*
and MLB.com. He'd been a must-read for me throughout high
school and college (in other words, as soon as I could read him
online), and his emphasis on history within his game stories
made him a hero of mine. Of course, it didn't hurt that he'd
provided a mentoring experience like few I'd had before or
since.

Back in 2007, during my first season covering the team for the *New York Observer*, I'd been working on a complicated story about Lastings Milledge and the press coverage he'd received. Unlike nearly every other beat reporter, Marty had introduced himself to me and provided a friendly hello during subsequent encounters in the press box or clubhouse. It may not sound like much, but particularly given the attitudes of other writers, it was soothing to a first-timer.

So in an effort to gain greater perspective on the Milledge piece, I asked Marty if he had a few minutes to discuss it. He said that he did, and would, as soon as he finished his work for the night. In the meantime, I waited for him in the clubhouse. Players packed up and left, and one by one the beat reporters did the same thing. Eventually, only Marty remained of all the credentialed media members. I saw him wear a path between the lockers of Aaron Heilman and David Wright, nailing down the details for what turned out to be his fifth filed story of the night with MLB.com. He'd been covering baseball since Mickey Mantle's final season, but of all the reporters, he managed to work the hardest that night. And yet he proceeded to walk with me to the Shea Stadium parking lot and answer every question I had about my story for the next twenty minutes.

I wondered: How would Marty see my campaign? He was from the old school of baseball journalism, the one that taught you never to show a rooting interest in the team you covered, or any other. I couldn't imagine letting go of the emotional hold the Mets' fortunes had on me, and respectfully disagreed with the idea that it should render me unable to analyze the team well. A fan did not mean a cheerleader, and in my role writing about the Mets, it behooved me to search every area for ways the Mets would either need to improve or were succeeding. Hoping they did had very little to do with how accurate my analysis was—as a fan, with the understanding that many people would be reading my work, my affinity for the team meant I had a larger stake in being right than someone who didn't care either way.

But I definitely wondered if Marty Noble would see it that way, or if he even thought my ideas about how to change the team made sense.

The experience overwhelmed me from the moment I entered the pizzeria, ducked around a corner, and took in the large crowd that had gathered. Mets memorabilia hung from the walls, and within the crowd I spotted a number of bloggers I'd spoken with over the phone and Internet: Metsgrrl's Caryn Rose, NJ.com's Matthew Artus, even Randy Medina, creator of the Apple, a humor site inspired by the Onion. Greg and his wife, Stephanie, sat in a corner booth, and up front by the microphone sat Marty Noble, like the king of all Met fandom. I shook hands and exchanged hellos without glad-handing—I liked people but hadn't mastered the politician's skill yet. I also hadn't prepared a speech. I didn't want to talk at the crowd—I wanted them to hear me, a Mets fan who cared as they did, and tell them why I believed we could change the course of how the Mets were run together.

I began by making the point that fan voting on the leadership of sports teams is relatively common in a number of other sports, soccer in particular. Members of Real Madrid, for a fee of around five hundred dollars, get the opportunity to vote for a team president, the rough equivalent of a general manager in baseball. Those members also have the right to purchase season tickets, but clearly a direct say in who runs the club is the draw. And presidential elections are open, raucous affairs, with candidates promising various moves if elected. The Red Sox, almost certainly inspired by the European model, created Red Sox Nation, including membership fees. They didn't offer fans a direct say in club affairs, but Theo Epstein almost certainly would be reelected for the foreseeable future. Here with the Mets, however, the stakes were quite different.

I looked around. Clearly, I had the crowd's attention. I began to lay out my vision for the team—the changes in basic draft philosophy, as well as the promise to allow injured players to heal without fear that the Mets would blame them for their own ailments. (This was basic but surprisingly not easy to get from the current team.) I stumped for a focus on reasonable, stat-savvy solutions instead of the big splash, and I saw something encouraging. To these beaten-down fans, hearing about what could be for the New York Mets—just hearing about it—seemed to provide hope. Little about the team's current play had mitigated my message, either. The Mets, since reaching their high-water mark at 43–32, had struggled to 5–8 since. Of course I knew that thirteen games meant very little, but still: The Mets were certainly not undercutting my arguments. Yes, Omar Minaya's Mets, like his predecessor's teams, were failing in a multitude of ways—but there was always tomorrow, and it could be brighter, and we could all go a long way toward making sure that it was.

Then we heard from Marty. And while much of his conversation was off-the-record, he confirmed plenty for all of us. That the team's penchant for needless secrecy went back several decades. That the lines of authority and communication were hopelessly tangled. That the doctors in charge of healing the Mets were more than competent—but the proper diagnoses were getting corrupted somewhere else. Somehow, thanks to Met mismanagement, players like Carlos Beltran and Jose Reyes not only missed much more time than the team thought they would, but the nature of their injuries changed, and eventually, Beltran even had surgery against the wishes of the Mets to try and correct a knee ailment. He regaled us with stories about players who'd managed to succeed for the Mets—Wally Backman and Tom Seaver and Gary Carter—and many who hadn't. And most important to me, he didn't seem to think any of my ideas were crazy or unworkable. Maybe he was being polite. But that's not really how Marty Noble works. If he thinks you are wrong, he tells you. When it came to diagnosing the team's ills, I wasn't wrong.

I returned home feeling triumphant. My message of LOGIC, TRANSPARENCY, and PASSION had translated with a group of fans as tuned into the operations and history of the New York Mets as any. Marty Noble hadn't gone all Joseph Welch on me. I felt more confident than ever that as the voting continued throughout the month, I'd only accumulate support.

The rest of July was a haze of escalating vote totals, interviews, middle-of-the-night diaper changes, and disappointing baseball from the Mets, who faded badly as the trade deadline approached. Keyed by my appearance at Grand Central, I won 71 percent of the vote from Faith and Fear in Flushing and 72 percent of the vote at NJ.com's Always Amazin'. Greg Prince and Matt Artus became two of my most vociferous supporters, with Greg's endorsement as eloquent as any I'd heard.

It's not a gag what Howard Megdal is doing. Oh, it's technically impossible. He can't run for general manager of the New York Mets, and he knows it. Well, he can run, but it's a non-binding election, a "beauty contest," as we political junkies would call those primaries that yield no delegates. Howard can gather all the victories on all the blogs that, like this one, are hosting his referendum, but even a clean sweep won't give him entrée to the front office at Citi Field.

Doesn't matter, though. The journey is the destination in Howard's case. The exercise alone is worthwhile (and not just because he plans to write a book about the experience). Howard will not be the general manager of the Mets in this life.

But he oughta be . . . Howard mentioned Monday at Two Boots that what he's doing isn't unprecedented in a sports context. Around the world, presidents of top soccer teams (Real Madrid, for example) are popularly elected. In Britain, "there's a movement on for more fan ownership of teams. The connection between a team and its fans is so significant in terms of time and energy that a more direct say by the fans makes a lot of sense . . . Besides," he adds, "we live in a representative democracy. Why should Mets fans in America be limited to spouting off on blogs and WFAN?

"This is not about results," he says. "The results will come once the process is in place." To Howard, the Mets have groped their way through recent seasons with no distinguishable process. Maybe process and planning would have won them a couple of extra games in 2007 and 2008. Maybe it would have prevented a total evaporation in 2009. And, beyond 2010, maybe it would mean a sturdier, steadier ship for the years ahead.

Howard's written some of this stuff before, either on his campaign Web site or in columns for sny.tv or nybaseball digest.com. Again, it's stuff we've all written give or take a detail here or there. But as a self-appointed candidate, he's truly articulated a vision. What he's doing may seem like a goof, but talk to him, Mets fan to Mets fan, and it's not goofy. It's inspiring.

Incredibly, this sentiment continued to spread. I began receiving e-mails and other messages of support from everywhere—a fan named Phil Coorey told me how much he was enjoying my campaign from Australia. I filmed a second commercial, this one about the mishandling of Jennry Mejia, in which I asked Mirabelle to perform tasks like drive a car or manage our investment portfolio to show the limits of rushing prospects. The ideas, and my campaign, seemed to be entering the bloodstream of the Mets.

It felt good, really good, to be heard.

While waiting on Mike Pelfrey after a late-July game in the Met clubhouse, the team's longtime PR director, Jay Horwitz, asked me: "When you get elected GM, will you hire me?" I assured him that I would. As luck would have it, Adam Rubin, the ESPN New York Mets beat reporter, happened to be standing right next to me. Rubin famously had been accused of trying to secure a position with the Mets through Omar Minaya the season before, at the press conference to announce Minaya's longtime associate Tony Bernazard's firing—which had been made necessary in the first place by Rubin's stellar reporting. I turned to Rubin and said, "Is it me, or did Jay just lobby for a job?"

Rubin looked right through me and said nothing. Apparently, we weren't laughing about that yet.

But Jay clearly had been seeing the vote totals as the summer continued. I received 67 percent support at Anthony De Rosa's Hot Foot blog. A week later, at Pick Me Up Some Mets, the blog of fiction writer and passionate Met fan Zoë Rice, I racked up an astounding 85 percent of the vote. That 85 percent of Mets fans could agree on anything shocked me; as Robert Kennedy said, "One fifth of the people are against everything all the time." By RFK's own math, I'd picked up a quarter of that group.

It was crazy to feel the optimism I was experiencing. Sure, the vote totals were staggering. But, as the critics of this project never tired of commenting, the votes by themselves didn't mean anything. Did I really think these online polls meant I was going to become GM? When I looked into my heart—yes, that's exactly what I thought. All we wanted, any of us, was something to believe in.

"Once upon a time, the Mets had a magical outfielder named Jeromy Burnitz," I whispered to Mirabelle at bedtime late in July. "And according to the newspaper Daddy read, *New York Mets Inside Pitch*, Burnitz could hit for power and also steal bases—he became the first farmhand in Mets history to go 30-30."

I could win all the primaries, I knew, and the Mets weren't obligated to follow my exhortations about anything. Not LOGIC. Not TRANSPARENCY. Not even PASSION.

"But before Burnitz had a chance to help the Mets, they decided to trade him for some pitching prospects named Paul Byrd, Dave Mlicki, and Jerry DiPoto," I continued. Mirabelle pawed at my cheek with less and less insistence as sleep began to take over. "Burnitz had six good seasons with Cleveland and Milwaukee, while Byrd, Mlicki, and DiPoto barely helped at all."

Sure, Deep Swoboda had been encouraging. But perhaps they'd decided to simply ignore me and continue operating as they always had.

"Finally, the Mets traded to get Burnitz back, giving up Benny Agbayani, pitcher Glendon Rusch, and other players, too. But by the time Burnitz came back to the Mets, all his speed was gone, and his mighty swing mostly led to strikeouts."

Still, something felt different. Baseball people believed in omens and superstitions: that mentioning a no-hitter would jinx it, that the Chicago Cubs were cursed, that certain players would always fail in key situations and others would always succeed. Bottom line: Something told me the Mets were listening this time.

"Finally, the Mets gave up on Burnitz again and traded him to the Dodgers for marginal prospects and some salary relief. The very next season, Jeromy Burnitz hit thirty-seven home runs."

Even this story didn't anger me as it once had. I placed my sleeping daughter in the crib and walked gingerly out of the nursery, smiling.

Still, with July 31 approaching, it was time to fear the worst from the current regime. The Mets displayed no real evidence that a massive turnaround was still possible; still, with the team hovering around four or five games out of a playoff spot, you knew they might make an aggressive trade to salvage the 2010 season. And though no one from the Mets would confirm it, Omar Minaya and Jerry Manuel both had to know their jobs were in jeopardy. Manuel certainly had been managing like it, playing veterans at the expense of younger players at every turn. (Never mind that when the veteran is Jeff Francoeur, more playing time isn't helping to save your job.) But the fear across much of the land settled on Omar Minaya: Would he make a similar trade, one that sacrificed what little young talent the Mets had for a small chance at 2010 glory?

There were two historical events that led to this fear, one involving Minaya, the other involving the Mets. For Omar, taking over GM duties of the Mets followed a period when he'd run things for the Montreal Expos. And, strange as this seems now, the Expos weren't expected to move to Washington after the 2004 season. It was expected that they'd cease to exist after the 2002 season.

Imagine this, if you will: A general manager has been told by Major League Baseball that his team will have no future. At that moment, there is no planning for next year. So on June 27, 2002, with Montreal six and a half games out in the NL East and five games out in the wild card-race, the Expos acquired Bartolo Colon from the Cleveland Indians for Cliff Lee, Brandon Phillips, Grady Sizemore, and Lee Stevens. It is the prospect-based package that every fan dreams of receiving and fears giving up. While Stevens was simply a decent-hitting first baseman (and no prospect), Cliff Lee became a Cy Young award winner (and the subject of trade hopes himself, assuming the Colon role). Brandon Phillips, upon arriving in Cincinnati (Cleveland didn't know what they had), became perennially one of the finest second basemen in the league. And until injuries slowed his career, Grady Sizemore was the envy of every team for his play in center field, both offensively and defensively—with the exception of Carlos Beltran and the Mets.

Colon pitched well for Montreal, but the Expos finished just 83–79. As we now know, Major League Baseball didn't contract them, and the Expos suddenly had a would-be free agent on their hands they couldn't afford. Just months after snagging him, Minaya dealt Colon to the White Sox in a three-team deal, landing Rocky Biddle, Orlando Hernandez, Jeff Liefer, and, most important, cash. The new players were neither prospects, nor did they provide Montreal with much immediate help. The entire thing was a debacle—not entirely Minaya's fault, to be sure, but a debacle.

The other source of paranoia from this generation of Mets fans came from a trade the Mets made around two years after Montreal acquired Colon. It was the July 30, 2004, trade of Scott Kazmir for Victor Zambrano, and, like a deal thirty-plus years before it in Mets history—Nolan Ryan for Jim Fregosi—it provides the essence of the smaller missteps that echoed from these two deals throughout New York Mets history.

Chapter 12

OUR TEAM, OUR TIME

I WASN'T ALIVE when the Mets traded Nolan Ryan for Jim Fregosi, so it is impossible for me to know how I'd have reacted. But I know how I felt at the moment—the very moment—I heard about the trade of Scott Kazmir for Victor Zambrano. The day before the deal occurred, the *New York Post* reported that it was in the works. And I was relieved to read it in the *Post*—the same paper that had assured me earlier that month that Richard Gephardt was John Kerry's running mate—because it simply had to be an invention. The Mets wouldn't possibly do such a thing. Not that I had a ton of faith in the Mets, mind you. But this was awful, even for them. A day later, Zambrano was a Met.

The Ryan-Fregosi and Kazmir-Zambrano trades have been mythologized by fans, but in reality neither was a straight player-for-player swap. Ryan was part of a five-player deal; in Kazmir's case, four players changed hands. Both trades involved the same mistakes and the same fan outrage, and each embodies the worst decision making the franchise is capable of. In each case, the

Mets traded a pitcher with tremendous talent at a very young age. But as previously discussed, pitching prospects aren't sure things. What makes each trade so unforgivable is that both Ryan and Kazmir were among the best prospects in baseball. And each time, the Mets received an absurdly small return.

Which one is worse? I have spent many hours pondering this question, debating it with friends, letting what should be restful nights filled with mind- and body-restoring sleep get hijacked by such thoughts. I can't decide. They both represent the Mets at their most self-destructive. And they'll live on in the public consciousness for decades to come.

Nolan Ryan came to the Mets as a twelfth-round pick in the 1965 amateur draft, the first in baseball history. Immediately, two characteristics popped up that would stay with Ryan, to some extent, for the duration of his career. He walked a lot of hitters. And he struck out more than nearly anyone, ever. It is a sad reality that the strikeout totals in his primary minor-league stop—Greenville, Single-A ball, 1966—have been lost to history. What we do know is that he threw 183 innings for the Greenville Mets, walking 135—or 6.2 per nine innings. We also know that despite this absurdly high walk rate, he finished with a 17–2 record and a 2.51 ERA. And we know, in the minor-league stops from which we do have his strikeout totals, that he struck out 17.8 batters per nine innings. So even without the precise number, we have plenty of evidence that tells us: Nolan Ryan was as good a bet as any young pitcher in baseball to eventually hold the major-league record for career strikeouts.

But naturally, that is only part of the story. Ryan was an intense competitor, endlessly fun to watch. He threw a prodigious number of innings, worked out like few men in baseball history, and knocked batters down with reckless abandon. He may have been the most uncomfortable pitcher to face in baseball history. Put it this way: One of the signature moments of his career—one memorialized with a photo on display in the Texas Rangers' clubhouse—is Ryan, at age forty-six, beating the living hell out of Robin Ventura, age twenty-six, who had charged the mound. That's who Nolan Ryan was.

Ryan's essential Ryan-ness was on display even in the first three innings he threw in the major leagues, at age nineteen for the 1966 Mets—three innings, three walks, six strikeouts. And in his first regular action, at age twenty-one in 1968, he threw 134 innings, starting and relieving, and struck out 133 batters while walking 75. That remained his role with the Mets through 1971, his age-twenty-four season. To that point, he'd walked 6.1 batters per nine innings in the major leagues, and struck out 8.7.

Pretty clearly, the Mets were worried about his walks. And on one level, that's easy to understand: He really threw a *lot* of balls. Ryan led the major leagues in walks, and it wasn't close. But he was also at least two years younger than the next twenty-five pitchers on that list. And even with his walks, he still managed to get guys out: His ERA was a relatively low 3.51, league average. The point is, he only needed to make some small adjustments, mental and physical, and the potential was there for him to be, you know, Nolan Ryan.

That's why his strikeout rate was so important. Ryan's mark, among pitchers with at least 500 innings pitched from 1968 to 1971, ranked second in all of baseball. The top eighteen is a virtual who's who of pitching at the time: Sudden Sam McDowell, followed by Ryan, Mickey Lolich, Tom Seaver, Bob Gibson,

Ferguson Jenkins, Luis Tiant, Andy Messersmith . . . you get the picture. Don Sutton is fifteenth. Steve Carlton is seventeenth. And Ryan was at least two years younger than everyone on that list, while besting all but one of them in strikeout rate.

Nolan Ryan had not yet become a star when the Mets traded him. But he possessed such electric pitches, such power with his fastball, that in today's game he would have been a big-money prospect with success written all over him. And hype or no hype, a team would need a damn good reason to trade a player like him. The Baltimore Orioles, a few years before, had traded a terrific young pitcher named Milt Pappas. It was justified; they got Frank Robinson in return.

But that's not who the Mets and general manager Bob Scheffing got. They got Jim Fregosi.

I'll be fair: Had the Mets acquired Jim Fregosi early in his career, the trade might have made at least a bit of sense. From ages twenty-one to twenty-eight, Fregosi played a stellar defensive shortstop, posted an OPS+ of 119, and made six All-Star teams in eight years. From 1963 to 1970, no shortstop came close. His defense was superb, his offense was the finest of anyone at his position, and his durability was close to unmatched. No, he didn't throw seven no-hitters, pitch until he was forty-seven, and set the major-league record for strikeouts, but he was a very good player in his day.

But the Mets didn't trade for the age-twenty-one-to-twenty-eight Fregosi. They traded for him in the winter following the 1971 season. After barely missing a game from 1963 to 1970, in 1971 he'd played in just 107 due to injuries. After posting that 119 OPS+ over eight seasons, his production fell to just 89. In other words, the Angels had driven this car hard and now were looking for someone to take it off their hands. And the Mets didn't check their Carfax.

Okay, you're saying—maybe the Mets wanted to get Fregosi while his stock was still low. He'd had a great career and a year of injuries and they saw an opportunity to get him cheap. Except the Mets didn't buy him cheap, not even close. They acquired Fregosi for Nolan Ryan *and three other players.*

Catcher Frank Estrada played only briefly in the major leagues. Lefty Don Rose, a solid pitching prospect himself, threw 42 encouraging innings for the Angels in 1972 before injuries wrecked his career. And outfielder Leroy Stanton gave five years of above-average offensive production, then hit 27 home runs for the Seattle Mariners in the team's first season. For teams starved for offense, as the midseventies New York Mets were, that would have come in handy.

Ryan, as you may know, went on to throw seven no-hitters, strike out 5,714 batters, and win 324 games, with his best three-year stretch coming immediately after leaving the Mets—not coincidentally, his age-twenty-five-to-twenty-seven seasons. Upon leaving the Mets, he lowered his walk rate, though not significantly—he still walked 5.5 batters per nine over his next seven years. But that was enough of a drop, along with a rise in the strikeout rate to 10.1—to make him the Hall of Fame pitcher he's known as today.

And Fregosi? Well, the Mets didn't get much of a bargain. In fact, unsurprisingly, his first year for the Mets resembled the year immediately before it. He put up an identical 89 OPS+, he hit .232 after hitting .233 with the Angels, he played in 101 games due to injury, and the Mets moved him to third base from shortstop, which made him even less valuable. That he did this while Ryan struck out 329 batters in his first season, 383 in his second, was an additional kick in the shins.

I'd prefer to chalk this up as a lesson learned—a primer in the meaning of valuing prospects, and, you know, not trading good pitchers for nothing. But evidently it wasn't even that.

The Mets drafted Scott Kazmir, a Texan with an overpowering fastball and propensity for the strikeout (sound familiar?) with the fifteenth pick in the 2004 MLB draft. Sent to Brooklyn, he struck out 17 batters per nine innings in his first professional experience at eighteen. By age twenty, he was striking out 10 per nine, with a 1.73 ERA, for Double-A Binghamton. His walk rate was a reasonable 3.1 per nine. No one had homered off of him. This was a pitching prospect at the height of his powers.

Kazmir entered the 2005 season as the seventh-best prospect in all of baseball, according to *Baseball America*. He ranked ahead of many future stars, including Hanley Ramirez, Matt Cain, Prince Fielder, and Chad Billingsley. The only pitcher ranked ahead of Kazmir was Felix Hernandez—or, as you know him, reigning AL Cy Young award winner "King" Felix Hernandez. Of course, by the time Hernandez cracked the majors, Kazmir was the property of the Tampa Bay Devil Rays.

As the 2004 Mets approached the July 31 non-waiver trade deadline, the team found itself hovering around the .500 mark. In a division in which no one had played particularly well, the Mets were just a few games out—only a game out of first on July 15, and three back as late as July 22. So two things were clear. One, the Mets weren't very good, certainly not a real contender for a championship. And two, maybe the division was mediocre enough that if they added a few short-term parts—not at the expense of the future, of course—perhaps they could steal a playoff berth. A low-risk, high-upside trade made sense. Not, to be clear, trading your number-one pitching prospect for a random assortment of middling players.

As the week went on, even the possibility of stealing a play-off berth seemed to fade. The Mets dropped further back in the standings—by July 26, the Monday before the Kazmir trade, they were six games out. That's not an impossible mountain to climb—but what reason did they have to think they would? They would get no closer than five games back that week, and by Friday were six games out as they headed into a three-game series with division leader Atlanta.

The Mets actually made two trades that day. In one, they dealt Ty Wigginton, Jose Bautista, and minor-league pitcher Matt Peterson to Pittsburgh for Kris Benson and Jeff Keppinger. In Benson, they acquired a former number-one overall pick who had disappointed in Pittsburgh and would go on to do the same in New York. Keppinger was a utility infielder, like Wigginton, with a below-average glove, like Wigginton, but without an above-average bat, unlike Wigginton. Bautista, of course, would go on to hit 54 home runs for the 2010 Blue Jays, not that anyone on any team expected that. But it still stings a little when you consider how little the Mets got in return.

And this trade is easily forgotten, dwarfed by the sheer magnitude of dealing Scott Kazmir and Joselo Diaz—a raw young arm—to Tampa Bay for Victor Zambrano and Barto-lome Fortunato, a nondescript reliever. Like Jim Fregosi thirty-three years earlier, Victor Zambrano was twenty-nine years old. And in the December 1971 deal, it had been bad enough that Nolan Ryan was twenty-four. In July 2004, Kazmir was only twenty.

Here's the story of the main return the Mets received for

one of the top prospects in all of baseball. Zambrano, set to turn thirty the week after the Mets got him, was coming off a 2003 season with a 4.21 ERA while leading the American League in walks, hit batsmen, and wild pitches. His control had actually regressed from that point in 2004, with his walk rate jumping to 6.8 per nine innings at the time of the trade. In fact, even though he pitched for Tampa Bay only through the end of July, he led the American League in walks in 2004 as well. In short, he was a project, about to turn thirty, meaning the chances that he'd amount to anything were virtually nil.

But Howard, you might say, didn't Nolan Ryan also have control problems? I'm glad you asked that question. He certainly did. He was also six years younger than Zambrano when the Mets traded him, and his strikeout rate, remember, was among the best in all of baseball. Zambrano, by comparison to the great Ryan, was old, wild, and, frankly, bad. Among pitchers with more than 400 innings pitched from 2001 to 2004, Zambrano's K rate ranked thirtieth, behind mediocrities like Kazuhisa Ishii, Adam Eaton, and Tony Armas Jr. He wasn't even first among Zambranos, trailing Carlos of the Cubs.

So the acquisition of a healthy Victor Zambrano for Scott Kazmir would rank among the most ridiculous choices the franchise ever made. There's just one more thing you should know.

Zambrano wasn't healthy. The Mets traded for damaged goods. And this, too, was their own fault. They chose not to do their own physical on Zambrano prior to acquiring him. As a result, three starts into his Mets tenure, Zambrano was lost for the season with an elbow injury. And in 2006, following a typical Zambrano season in 2005 (4.17 ERA, boatload of walks), he ran off the mound in his fifth start, holding his elbow.

Tommy John surgery ended his season and his tenure with the Mets.

As of this writing, it would appear that the Mets did not give up another Nolan Ryan in Scott Kazmir. Tampa Bay, which wasn't run particularly well back then, rushed him straight to the major leagues in 2004, where he showed promise, then increased his innings load significantly in 2005, when he was Tampa Bay's best pitcher. From 2005 to 2008 he was one of baseball's best, with an ERA+ of 128 and 9.7 strikeouts per nine innings. Most painful of all for Mets fans, a Kazmir in the 2006 rotation probably means a win over the Cardinals in the NLCS and a trip to the World Series. A Kazmir in the 2007 and 2008 rotations probably means a playoff berth each season. Though injuries slowed him down in 2009 and 2010, Kazmir's worth over four seasons would have been huge for any team: For the Mets, it may have meant an unprecedented level of success. It's hard not to think, as you look back over the wreckage of this trade, that he might've brought his team a championship.

But it was not to be. There wasn't a sea of Kazmir jerseys at Shea, no World Series, no multiple playoff appearances. Instead there was the infuriating tenure of Victor Zambrano.

And the craziest part is, the moment the Mets made the Kazmir trade, *everyone* knew they'd been fleeced. This isn't twenty-twenty hindsight. I was living in upstate New York, and my parents had come to visit. I just remember the whole night as dark. I remember telling my father about the trade through the dingy screen door that led to my first apartment. I remember the dimly lit living room, where we watched the Mets fall seven games back over takeout Chinese food. The entire weekend has a pall over it in my memory—even the sunlit Sunday afternoon when my parents headed back to South Jersey, following a sweep by Atlanta that left New York nine games back and hopelessly out of the race, three days into the Victor Zambrano Win-Now Era.

And as the non-waiver trade deadline approached in 2010, so did the fear that a Mets management team on the ropes would do the same thing once again.

Chapter 13

YES WE CAN

DRIVING ALONG IN late July, a roadside sign caught me up short: SPANISH LESSONS AGE 6 MOS. AND UP, followed by a phone number. This came on the heels of getting solicited, at a jazz concert, for a program to introduce children to jazz at ages eight months and older. With Mirabelle now four months old, the world was coming for my daughter.

This was exciting, of course. I wanted her to experience these things. I'd been feeding her a steady diet of formula and adjusted pitching stats, but that didn't mean I wanted her to turn into some kind of baseball savant, unwilling or unable to enjoy anything else. I wanted her to hear great music, to speak confidently in what appeared to be the country's most vital second language, and to know about the world outside her own. I admit it: Sometimes her bedtime stories came from sections other than Sports in the *New York Times*. But these special baby classes and opportunities were the beginning of a lifelong onslaught—basically, an international conspiracy to fill up poor Mirabelle's schedule. And before I lost her to text messages, Facebook, and baby Pilates, I had something I wanted to do with my daughter: bring her to her first game at Citi Field. On July 31, 2010, the moment arrived.

I knew it would be vital to strike a proper balance with Mirabelle, somewhere between how to turn your head toward home plate and when to call in a lefty specialist in a high-leverage inning. I knew the refrain from Calvin Trillin, my primary source on child-rearing—that when exposing children to new things, "Less is more." I had no intention of making baseball into some kind of knowledge test; the reason I yearned to share it with my daughter, at long last, was that it provided an unending source of pleasure even when our favorite team lost.

But I also knew what a disservice I'd be doing to her by oversimplifying baseball. She'd become a veteran of my baseball stories, had been hearing games since she was in the womb. Schools are filled with kids who hate one subject or another, not because of a lack of aptitude but because their skills are far beyond those being taught. Without false modesty, if my genetic predispositions were any indication, Mirabelle would be expecting more from the ballpark than cotton candy and glam-rock anthems. (If only a few more Mets managers had been the same way . . .)

Mirabelle didn't look away from me when I explained to her about the pitching matchup that afternoon at lunch. Yes, she stuck her hands in my mouth, but her attention never wavered. It wouldn't be fair to say that Rachel and I were working at cross purposes, but while Rachel had been encouraging Mirabelle to make *M-m-m* and *D-d-d* sounds, presaging *Mommy* and *Daddy*, I'd been hell-bent on getting her first words to be *Hisanori Takahashi*. So far we'd both fallen short, which, as I pointed out to Rachel, made it just as likely that Mirabelle would name the Japanese hurler on the mound that night as simply addressing either of us.

But before I could take my family to Citi Field—this, as far as I could tell, was the primary purpose in having a family—I had work to do. Mirabelle wasn't *ready* to enter this environment, not while I was still so upset about how it was being managed. And time was running out for her, too, because I couldn't deprive her of the ballpark experience much longer, not without risking substantial psychological damage. If I couldn't take over the team before her first game, I certainly wasn't going to let her believe it would always be this way.

I needed to let the national public know exactly how the Mets would operate under the Megdal administration. I'd been approached by ESPN.com to deliver what amounted to a State of the Union response to whatever Omar Minaya did or didn't do to improve the Mets by the non-waiver trade deadline. This was my time to communicate with my daughter.

Naturally, the piece needed to be essentially forward-thinking. I was limited in some ways, because I had no way of knowing which contracts the Mets were letting Minaya terminate, nor how much they were willing to spend. I had a lot of specific ideas but would have to write a much more generalized piece. Still, it was clear what I'd made myself in the eyes of many: the Alternative.

Armed with that knowledge, and anticipating that evening's baseball game with Rachel and Mirabelle, I sat in front of my computer and composed a message to the public.

With the passing of the non-waiver trading deadline at four P.M. this past Saturday, the problems of the New York Mets, a team that has failed to leverage star players performing superbly into playoff appearances and championships, were allowed to crystallize further.

No magic trade manifested itself; the dreams of adding Dan Haren, Roy Oswalt, or any reasonable alternative to Luis Castillo at second base tragically went unrealized. That is to be expected: There is no deus ex machina moment in the running of a major-league baseball team.

The Mets have often erred by looking for a magic trade at various points in their recent history instead of applying LOGIC, TRANSPARENCY, and PASSION. As a result, most of the same problems that kept the Mets one game shy of the playoffs in 2007 and 2008 continue to plague the roster.

Hope, quickly dashed by despair, should not be the plight of Mets fans, young and old, around the world. Therefore I am running for general manager of the New York Mets, because I believe no child in blue-and-orange footie pajamas should go to bed hungry for quips to throw at Yankees fans the next day at school. No child of the Mets should grow up wondering what October baseball feels like.

I continued by diagnosing particular problems—second base, the outfield, the rotation, the bullpen. All of my solutions carried more caveats than I'd have preferred. But I simply wasn't willing to make promises based on information I didn't yet have. However, changes to benefit the fans directly were a far easier case to make. I concluded with this:

For example, there will be a return to such traditions as Banner Day, Old-Timers' Day, and Helmet Day. Theme dates will provide entertainment value and a gift people actually want to take home. The Mets will no longer limit giveaways to "the first 25,000 fans" or, worse, "the first 5,000 fans 12 and under," leaving some children who might be attending their first Mets game with the twin disappointment of getting stuck in traffic, then getting to watch other children play with the toy they were too late to receive.

New promotions will be introduced. Much as Broadway shows often have "student rush" seats, the Mets should put aside a few sections right behind home plate—the ones near the field that cost way too much—and let anyone with a valid student ID purchase a seat in them for $10 apiece on the day of the game. For a temporary tiny revenue loss, the Mets get the advantage of reaching out to their youngest fans, making potential customers for decades. They also make it clear that, unlike their rivals across town, the Mets aren't looking to milk fans for every last dollar. Best of all, what is now a tomblike feel to the area closest to the playing field will become a raucous home-field advantage for the team and a three-hour advertisement during every ballgame for how much fun it is to come to Citi Field.

I'm in it for the construction worker who nearly falls off his support beam after hearing the Mets hit into a game-ending, unassisted triple play. I'm in it for the single mother of four who finally puts her children to bed, only to watch the Mets bullpen blow another lead. I'm in it for the senior living on a fixed income who takes his morning pills at night in a confused rage after seeing Jerry Manuel bunt with his cleanup hitter. And I'm in it, maybe most of all, for the crying child—crying because she had to watch John Maine pitch.

I urge you all to join my crusade for change with the Mets. Remember, the Wilpons have never hesitated to spend money on this baseball team. We need to make sure that the frustration that every one of us feels in seeing it spent fruitlessly stops. Each day brings us closer to this horrific reality: that the peak performances of the two best players this organization has produced in decades will go to waste.

When I join you in the stands to watch David Wright's 5 and Jose Reyes' 7 join the other retired numbers on the Citi Field left-field wall, I want the scoreboard to play highlights from their many postseason runs. Elect me, and we as Mets fans don't have to play the fifty-year game we've all engaged in: What Might Have Been?

I'd stated my case, as clearly and forcefully as I knew how. And now, with the knowledge that my child's future was wide open, it was time to go enjoy a baseball game.

We'd taken Mirabelle many places by now—the park, her baby naming, family get-togethers—so making certain we had all the necessary amenities was relatively easy. She'd had a bottle around four P.M., so, assuming her normal schedule, she'd eat around seven thirty and probably start to fade at eight or eight fifteen. We weren't planning on watching a full game, which was a new experience for me. I just didn't leave games early, ever. If the Mets led by a lot, I wanted to see them celebrate. If they trailed by a lot, I knew, by leaving, that I'd be denying myself the chance to witness one of the all-time best comebacks. If they trailed by even more, I might get to see something truly rare, like a position player pitching.

But we were in unknown territory. Mirabelle had never been in a place with so many other people. How would she react? It was entirely possible that we'd get to Citi Field and she'd be afraid, start crying, and that would be the end of our endeavor. I steeled myself for this possibility, even though I'd been dreaming of walking into Citi Field with her since before Citi Field existed—and before she existed. I'd even made a video of a 2008 game with Rachel at Shea Stadium, taking a tour of the premises, with narration directed toward my future, as-yet-unconceived child. If it had to wait, though, it had to wait.

I don't mean this as a shot at other, lesser babies, but we are extremely lucky with how easy and cooperative Mirabelle is. She travels extraordinarily well, and she was relaxed as we hit the typical Whitestone Bridge traffic. We arrived at Citi Field around six thirty—early enough to park, take in a few sights, grab the necessary Mama's of Corona sandwich (turkey and mozzarella), and arrive at our seats. I'd chosen those with care—directly behind home plate, Promenade Box, allowing for easy entrance/exit and parking of Mirabelle's stroller. And yes—I got them from StubHub. Better seats. Lower prices.

It was finally happening. The funny thing is, I could feel more than just the single moment as the three of us entered below the huge mural of Gil Hodges—a man my father had rooted for when Hodges was a slugging first baseman with the Brooklyn Dodgers and my father was a child, and again later when Hodges was a manager of the New York Mets and Dad was a collegian. As we walked through the turnstiles, I could feel the moment I'd lived so many times with my father—the excitement of receiving a Juan Samuel glove, courtesy of Tastykake, as a Veterans Stadium giveaway, then the thrill of seeing him traded to the Mets, followed by the disappointment of seeing him actually play for the Mets.

We walked into the VIP entrance on the first-base side, found ourselves an elevator (unlike the ones at Shea Stadium, these moved from floor to floor in less than the time it takes to conduct a therapy session), and surprisingly quickly procured our sandwiches and found our seats. An inning later, I'd eaten, Mirabelle had eaten, and it was time to let her sit on my lap and take in the game.

Sure, the ultimate outcome didn't matter all that much— but I'd happily seen to it that the Mets faced the Diamondbacks, the NL's worst team, for Mirabelle's debut game. A little good mojo never hurts.

Rachel had taken great care to make certain I had reasonable expectations for the entire experience. "Just letting Mirabelle see and feel the park will be worthwhile," she cautioned. "She may not last long." I'd agreed with Rachel intellectually, but in my mind this only went one way—Mirabelle, on my lap, talking baseball with me. And that's exactly what happened.

I'd like to think the periodic stares we got came from passersby who were in awe of Mirabelle's concentration powers. (Chances are, they were probably wondering why I'd just told an infant, "Don't worry, Barry Enright's success against the Mets tonight is largely an illusion built on unsustainable luck from balls in play.") They were right to be, of course—she happily took in the game, inning after inning, like a proper baseball fan. None of this Kids Korner–type nonsense for her. A baseball game was taking place directly in front of us. Who needed, or even wanted, other distractions?

Hisanori Takahashi did his part, striking out 10 batters over 6 innings (though she did not speak his name). This allowed me to expose Mirabelle to the simple effectiveness of changing pitch speeds, with the vital lesson sinking in that the pitcher who throws hardest isn't necessarily the one who succeeds most. But the night was filled with firsts. Her first RBI came, appropriately enough, from David Wright. The second came from the bat of Jose Reyes. Perfect. She got to see Takahashi sacrifice bunt. Angel Pagan doubled, the ball bouncing once and landing over the wall in right-center, and I got to explain the concept of a ground-rule double. No home runs, but that was a lesson itself—baseball has entirely too many thrills to worry about whether your team hits a home run or not.

The well-pitched game and resulting pace meant we hit 8:30 right around the seventh inning. Mirabelle, for her part, had settled in nicely on my lap. Usually, I made sure to share her with Rachel—it seemed unfair to keep the baby, even though I found it nearly impossible to pass her off to anyone while she was smiling, which was almost always. But Rachel, ever the good soldier, had freely given up lap rights for the duration of the evening in exchange for future considerations and the right to take a paparazzi-like number of photos.

Takahashi departed after six innings and the Mets brought on Bobby Parnell for the top of the seventh. Mirabelle seemed to sense the tension throughout the stadium, since Parnell, in a rare off-day, didn't have it. She squeezed my thumb tightly with her entire hand as we watched Parnell and a succession of relievers turn a 2–1 Mets lead into a 4–2 deficit. As the inning ended, it became clear that at least part of Mirabelle's squeezing efforts came not from the game itself, but from her personal efforts to fill her diaper.

I knew it was time to clean her and go. She still sat, happily taking in the game and smiling at passers-by who said hello. Like a tiny, pink-bow-wearing Bob Feller, she'd have gone nine if I'd let her. But I needed to be responsible about such things. And it excited me more than reasonably that my daughter hadn't hit the showers early—she'd kept at it for as long as I'd let her—and I wasn't about to overextend her young arms (or legs or body or head).

I'll never forget her smiling face when I lifted her into the air during the middle of the seventh, seeing her stretch as if we were playing the now-familiar game Baby Airplane, smiling at me as I sang "Take Me Out to the Ballgame" to her. Sure, we missed the end of a baseball game for the first time in my life. The Mets tied it at four; we were busy cleaning Mirabelle up in the family restroom. By the time we'd taken our last photos outside of Citi Field, it was the eighth inning. By the time we reached the Whitestone Bridge, Mirabelle having fallen asleep in the car around Linden Avenue, just blocks from the stadium, the Mets mounted their winning rally. There was no risk that playing the game on the car radio would wake her; the sound of a Mets game, of Howie Rose shouting, "Put it in the books!" had become her lullaby.

All I knew was that the experience of watching baseball, live, with my wife and daughter had been one of the greatest I'd ever had. I immediately began to figure out how to get Mirabelle back to the stadium. And would she remember this night, or any subsequent one, several years from now? Unlikely.

This one was for me. But I was more determined than ever to see to it that the Mets we'd see for years to come provided happy endings like the one at the end of Mirabelle's first night at Citi Field. I wanted her to have a team like the 1986 Mets, the greatest collection of talent Mets fans ever saw.

Chapter 14

CAMELOT

OKAY, I UNDERSTAND this isn't typical—but I tend to have the same reaction to looking at a statistical summary of the 1986 New York Mets that construction workers have when a woman in a short skirt walks by. I linger on each number. I'd whistle at my computer screen if I knew how to whistle. (No, Lauren Bacall, you don't just put your lips together and blow. That's a very different sound.)

The team could do it all. They could hit for power. They could get on base. They could steal bases. They played good defense, especially at the most important positions. And holy hell, could they ever pitch. But almost as important, the team was a beautiful balance of veterans and young players given a chance. It had depth on the bench and in the bullpen. The '86 Mets could hurt you with lefties, with righties, with switch-hitters. I'm sorry; if you're a red-blooded baseball fan, you can't see the 1986 Mets on paper and not feel the temptation to catcall.

And that was just on paper. In live Technicolor, the team was, incredibly, better than the sum of its parts. Again and again those Mets trailed, only to come back and win. And that's not to say they were always trailing; a team with that kind of starting pitching often went ahead early and stayed there. When they were ahead, they usually won. And when they trailed, they often won anyway. That's how you run a record of 108–54, then win a World Series.

And as should come as no surprise to you by now, this kind of team didn't get slapped together with some duct tape and a few hasty trades. This was six years in the making, the finest hour of Frank Cashen, who was the best general manager the Mets ever had.

Cashen took over in 1980, the hire of new owners Nelson Doubleday and Fred Wilpon. The organization he inherited had very little talent, either at the major-league level or deeper in the system. Despite my many complaints about the 2010 team, Cashen faced a far more difficult task than the one I was seeking to take on myself. And by 1986, not only was the major-league team without peer in baseball: The minor-league system was teeming with prospects ready to take the major leaguers' places.

Just how loaded was this team? For starters, look at its bench. These were the players who couldn't get everyday places in Davey Johnson's lineup; still, he was a smart enough manager to get them plenty of at-bats. You can argue that the bench of the 1986 Mets had more talent than the starting lineups of most NL competitors. They had Mookie Wilson, age thirty, capable of quality defense in center field, a 115 OPS+, 25 stolen bases, and 9 home runs. They had a twenty-four-year-old Kevin Mitchell, who played every position in the outfield and infield but second base, posted a 124 OPS+, and hit 12 home runs. Just three years later he'd win a National League MVP, hitting 47 home runs. They had a twenty-five-year-old Howard Johnson, who played third base and shortstop, put up a 118 OPS+, and hit 10 home runs in just 220 at-bats. The following year he'd post the first of three 30-30 seasons. Their fifth outfielder was Danny Heep and his 123 OPS+. Their backup catcher was Ed Hearn, who provided plus defense and a 98 OPS+—about average for a catcher. They reacquired the former Met Lee Mazzilli in August, in time to get a 137 OPS+ out of him as a pinch hitter.

These were the players who couldn't make the everyday lineup. So where did Cashen get his all-star team of reserves? In Mookie Wilson he had one of the few gifts left over from the previous regime—a second-round pick in the 1977 draft. Kevin Mitchell had been an undrafted free agent from California. Cashen traded Walt Terrell, a starting pitcher he knew wouldn't crack his own rotation, to Detroit for Howard Johnson. Heep came to the Mets after the 1982 season in exchange for an undistinguished pitcher named Mike Scott. That Scott would, three years later, learn the split-fingered fastball and become a force in his thirties is a hard mistake to pin on Frank Cashen. Heep, however, continued his role as an outfielder and strong bat off the bench. Hearn signed as a minor-league free agent; the Mets, in essence, got him for nothing. (True to Cashen form, he eventually traded Hearn to Kansas City to land David Cone.) And Mazzilli was an in-season pickup after he was released by the Pirates.

So for those keeping score at home, that's one draft pick, an undrafted amateur, a minor-league free agent, a released veteran, and two low-risk trades. In every case, Cashen was dealing from a position of strength: unafraid to let go of a talented player, but never in a situation where he couldn't afford to lose them. Scott was fungible, and Terrell had talent but wasn't as good as Dwight Gooden, Ron Darling, Sid Fernandez, or other pitchers in the system. That depth enabled Cashen to make his move for HoJo, who became one of the most potent offensive weapons the Mets had for the next half decade. His power was startling, and I made certain I never missed a Howard Johnson at-bat, not merely because we shared a first name. His home runs were sudden explosions; with his compact swing, it seemed strange when the ball didn't leave the park once in the air.

The starting lineup, of course, was built in much the same fashion. Wally Backman was the other draft pick from the pre-Cashen era to help the 1986 Mets. He platooned at second base with Tim Teufel, whom Cashen acquired from Minnesota for a trio of unwanted prospects: Bill Latham, Joe Klink, and Billy Beane. (Yes, that one.) Ray Knight was a similar buy-low candidate to play third base: The Mets got him in August of 1984 for another three unwanted prospects: Gerald Young, Manuel Lee, and Mitch Cook. None of these six prospects would have had any place on the 1986 Mets.

Knight always struck me as the anti–Jim Fregosi. In both cases, the Mets sought a third baseman about thirty years old who'd been around 10 to 15 percent better than the league-average hitter but struggled mightily the year before they traded for him. In Fregosi's case, the price was Nolan Ryan and three other prospects. In Knight's case, the price was a speed-only outfielder in Young and two even lesser pieces. It says everything about the difference between the Mets in 1971 and the Mets under Frank Cashen.

As for the rest of the crew, Darryl Strawberry was Cashen's reward for taking over such a woebegone franchise—he was the top pick in Cashen's first draft. He was my favorite Met;

I still remember crying the day he left as a free agent. We were both tall for our age, both left-handed, with media members and schoolteachers, respectively, saying we weren't working up to potential.

Lenny Dykstra also came through the draft—a shrewd thirteenth-round pick in 1981. Rafael Santana was released by the Cardinals, who had no need for a shortstop with Ozzie Smith around, and the Mets willingly picked him up. George Foster, the left fielder, didn't last the 1986 season. He'd been acquired from Cincinnati in one of the few Cashen missteps— for swingman Greg Harris and two other bit players, pitcher Jim Kern and catcher Alex Trevino. But here, again, Cashen's surplus talent in the organization allowed him to take a chance on Foster, who'd just put up a 150 OPS+ with the Reds when the Mets traded for him. And the ample alternatives he had in left field allowed him to jettison Foster in 1986 when the Mets no longer needed him.

As for the two biggest names in the Met lineup, Keith Hernandez and Gary Carter, Cashen took advantage of a combination of things. For one, the fact that he'd collected so much young talent meant that when Hernandez and Carter hit the trade market, he could outbid competitors without damaging the depth of his major-league club or farm system. When unique talents like Carter and Hernandez become available—in both cases, arguably the finest players in the National League at each position—you pounce. For another, Cashen kept doing what he always did: dealing from depth. The players he gave up in the Hernandez and Carter deals had ready-made replacements. And no Met fan can forget the pleasure of seeing Gary Carter gun down opposing runners, or the cerebral perfection of Keith Hernandez's approach at the plate or his perfect swing. As for his glove? Well, no one had ever played first base like Hernandez, and no one has since. On my *1986 Mets: A Year to Remember* video, he makes this play way up the first-base line, where he gathers the ball in while making a forward roll into right field. It catches me up short every time—and trust me, that is a well-worn VHS tape.

In Hernandez's case, when the St. Louis Cardinals decided they'd had enough of the twenty-nine-year-old Gold Glove–winning first baseman (who, in their defense, had struggled with a drug problem), the Mets happily snapped him up for the price of closer Neil Allen and minor-league pitcher Rick Ownbey. In each case, the Mets knew they had better alternatives. Sure, Allen was twenty-five and threw hard, but Jesse Orosco was also twenty-five, had better command, and missed more bats. And Ownbey would hardly be missed in the sea of prospects with better minor-league numbers.

The calculation with Gary Carter was even more airtight. The haul the Mets had given up on December 10, 1984, to bring in the best catcher in baseball was Hubie Brooks, Mike Fitzgerald, Herm Winningham, and Floyd Youmans. In Brooks, the Mets had a player who played third base and a bit of shortstop, about to turn twenty-eight years old. He'd put up a respectable OPS+ of 92 over five seasons, including 114 in 1984. But *three days earlier*, in what had to be part of a two-step maneuver, Cashen had acquired Howard Johnson—who played third base and a bit of shortstop, hit for more power than Brooks, and was four years younger. In other words, he'd already upgraded from the man who became the centerpiece of the Gary Carter trade.

As for the others? Fitzgerald was a young, defense-first catcher, entirely replaceable. Ultimately, Ed Hearn was equal to what the Mets could expect from Fitzgerald. Anyhow, he wouldn't have a chance to start in New York—thanks to Gary Carter. Herm Winningham was a speed-first outfielder, nowhere near the talent level of Dykstra, Mitchell, Strawberry, or even Wilson or Heep. And Floyd Youmans was a solid second-round draft pick—but finished fourth on his own single-A team's rotation in strikeout rate. In Double-A, just prior to getting traded, he was overshadowed by Rick Aguilera, Roger McDowell, Randy Myers, and Calvin Schiraldi. The first three pitched for the 1986 Mets. The fourth helped them to land their best-performing pitcher—and, as a bonus, gave up the go-ahead home run in Game 7 of the World Series to Ray Knight. This being a Cashen team, you could almost believe he'd planned that, too.

But that pitching was the essence of what made the 1986 Mets great. Of course, they did lead the National League in runs scored and manage a team-wide OPS+ of 106—higher than Jose Reyes's career figure—which is to say their lineup, collectively, was above average. But when your pitching is every bit as good as that hitting, it does explain how you finish 108–54.

In 1986 the Mets had the best ERA in the National League, even adjusting for park—and the youngest pitching staff in the league, with an average age of twenty-five and a half. The top nine pitchers in innings logged were twenty-nine or younger; the rotation boasted only a single pitcher older than twenty-five. That's how impressive the young pitchers were that Frank Cashen had assembled—arguably, greater than even the 1969 group. And once again he didn't simply collect pitching prospects in one particular way—he got them in every way possible.

The team's ace, Dwight Gooden (17–6, 2.84 ERA), came via the fifth overall pick in the 1982 draft. (An astounding fifteen players Cashen drafted in 1982 eventually played in the major leagues.) Gooden dominated the minor leagues to a greater extent than even Scott Kazmir or Nolan Ryan. But Frank Cashen didn't trade him—he put him at the top of his rotation in 1984 and kept him there for a decade. Sadly, only substance abuse kept that tenure from lasting even longer. Really, I only fully understood what it meant to watch Gooden dominate once he was gone. I simply knew him as the best of a talented bunch with the 1986 Mets, and at age six had nothing for comparison. Now, after two decades of Mauro Gozzo, Pete Smith, and Kazuhisa Ishii . . . I get it.

Gooden's 1986 was actually bested by a pair of his rotation mates. Bob Ojeda (18–5, 2.57 ERA) came to the Mets from the Red Sox prior to the 1986 season in a seven-player deal, where only Ojeda and the aforementioned Schiraldi amounted to much in the major leagues. Cashen recognized that his team was ready to win; he cashed in the prospect Schiraldi for the proven lefty Ojeda. Schiraldi went on to a very good career, but Cashen nailed the timing perfectly: Ojeda was just twenty-eight, helped them win a World Series, and gave them several more good years afterward.

He also acquired Ron Darling (15–6, 2.81 ERA) in a trade. That deal, made back in 1982 with the Rangers, provides a window into how effective Cashen was at seeing future value instead of past value. He traded fan favorite Lee Mazzilli, who'd been a bright spot for the god-awful Mets, for Darling and Walt Terrell. Both pitchers had succeeded at Double-A, so Cashen knew they'd likely be ready for major-league action sooner than later. Darling improved his strikeout rate at Triple-A and became a rotation horse. Terrell regressed a bit at Triple-A, so Cashen traded him for HoJo. By the time 1986 rolled around,

Mazzilli was available on the waiver wire, anyway. And of course Darling also proved to my mother that I could go to Yale and still hope to pitch for the Mets.

Cashen used Double-A success as a guide to help him evaluate Sid Fernandez (16–6, 3.52) as well. He'd been a third-round pick of the Dodgers in 1981. Evidently the Dodgers saw his 5.6 walks per nine innings in Double-A and wanted to cash him in—Cashen saw a pitcher who'd struck out 12.3 per nine as a twenty-year-old at Double-A and knew he had a potential rotation stalwart on his hands. The Fernandez deal is crazy one-sided—the Mets got him and Ross Jones, a utility infielder, for Bob Bailor, a utility infielder six years older than Jones, and Carlos Diaz, a lefty reliever Cashen sold high. Fernandez and his strikeout rate translated well to the major leagues, and El Sid pitched effectively with the Mets for a decade. He was one of my favorites, with a rising fastball that befuddled hitters and a waistline that didn't make you think of the word *athlete*. The stature of David Wells, with better stuff and a sweeter disposition.

As for the rest, Cashen simply let the draft and natural attrition do their work—with the caveat, of course, that he employed a scouting department as good as anybody's to find that talent. Rick Aguilera, the fifth starter, was a third-round pick in 1983. Righty co-closer Roger McDowell was a third-round pick in 1982; lefty co-closer Jesse Orosco was the rare gift left over from the previous regime—in an odd bit of organizational symmetry, the Mets acquired him back in 1978 for Jerry Koosman. Orosco, of course, was the pitcher for the final out of the 1986 World Series; Koosman was the pitcher on the mound for the final out of the 1969 World Series (getting 1986's manager Davey Johnson to fly out). Doug Sisk? Amateur free agent. Randy Myers? First-round draft pick, 1982. The Mets didn't go for the expensive fix in their bullpen; they made certain the organization was filled with young pitching talent, and the starters who didn't develop well enough to make the rotation—guys like Myers and McDowell—became top relievers instead.

There are so many clear lessons in the way the 1986 Mets were built, it is hard to imagine how the Mets failed to follow them in the more than two decades since. For one thing, notice that Cashen, for all of his transactions, didn't utilize the big-ticket free agent at all. This reflects less Cashen's philosophy and more the team's philosophy at large for much of the time free agency has existed. Still, two conclusions are obvious: It is distinctly possible to build a team without free agency, and the multiple draft picks usually given up in pursuit of a big-ticket free agent are often far more useful to a team, particularly in the hands of a talented scouting director. In the case of the Mets, that was Joe McIlvane from 1981 to 1985. Not coincidentally, he also built the team that won 88 games or more from 1997 to 2000 for Steve Phillips; he'd been the GM of the Mets from 1994 to 1997.

What else can we glean? Well, the Mets' average age was exactly twenty-eight, sixth in the National League. But notice that the team's success was built primarily on players younger than twenty-eight (Gooden, Strawberry, Dykstra, Backman, Darling, Fernandez), while the team went with established veterans sparingly and only when the available alternatives weren't close to the same talent level—in other words, Keith Hernandez and Gary Carter.

In addition, Cashen, in pursuit of talent, laid waste to the idea that he'd build a team with any particular theme. His offense had power hitters like Carter and Strawberry, more well-rounded offensive players like Hernandez, Knight, and Dykstra, and some hackers like Wilson and Backman. His pitchers could be tall and thin like Ron Darling or rotund and cuddly like Sid Fernandez. His players gained a reputation as hard-nosed, gritty players, yet finished at the very bottom of the National League in stolen base attempts and barely ever sacrificed. Instead, they got that reputation for coming back, again and again—the twin results of a potent offense and strong bullpen, not some magic combination of small-ball baseball tactics.

Somehow, all of this is lost to history. The 1986 Mets, in many memories, are Wally Backman bunting. But his 14 sacrifice bunts are, by far, the most of any regular player—only Lenny Dykstra, of the other Mets, had more than three. They are a team that did whatever it took to win, and usually that meant waiting for the three-run homer. In fact, even the roster itself took years to put together—it is that very patience, rather than urgency, that drove the Mets to their most successful season.

And while that 1986 season represents the only championship, keep in mind that from 1984 to 1990, the Mets were an elite team. They won 100 games and the National League East in 1988, only to be upset by the Los Angeles Dodgers, a team they'd beaten ten of eleven times in the regular season, in the National League Championship Series. They won 90 games in 1984, 98 games in 1985, 92 games in 1987, 87 games in 1989, and 91 games in 1990. Had the three-division wild-card format been in place back them, they'd have made the playoffs every single season from 1984 to 1990. There's never been any period of success like it in the team's history. Nothing close.

I don't view those years as a disappointment, even though many people do, considering that all that talent led to only a single championship. That is the limitation of baseball—there are no guarantees. Not for the Yankees, and certainly not for the Mets. It was up to a general manager to put the organization in position to achieve consistent success. If the ball bounced the right way, championships would follow. So I had my blueprint. I knew exactly the plan I'd outline for the Wilpons. And increasingly, the voters seemed determined to give me that chance.

Chapter 15

THE PEOPLE HAVE SPOKEN

A UGUST OF 2010 meant a lot of things to the Megdal household. Mirabelle began to laugh regularly, instantly voiding any part of my humor repertoire that wouldn't work on a five-month-old. The Mets followed a 9–17 July with a 12–16 August, dropping them out of the pennant race and making a change at the general manager position far more likely. Still, the attendant pleasures in writing about baseball remained in place; extended conversation with R. A. Dickey, for instance, more than passed the time, while the trade of Jeff Francoeur to the Texas Rangers and the release of Alex Cora continued to pro-vide hope that the Mets could learn from their mistakes or, at least, know that it was time to stop the bleeding.

Meanwhile, the more time I had to present my ideas to Mets fans, the more likely they seemed to respond to them. James Blind of the fan site the Happy Recap had me on for an hour-long program and grilling to kick off voting there; I managed to win 88 percent of the vote. Over at Mets Police, the fan watchdog Shannon Shark's site, I garnered more than 73 per-cent of the vote. And so it continued. Andrew Vazzano's the

'Ropolitans voted Megdal at a 76 percent clip. I was now up to eleven wins in eleven primaries, and it really was beginning to feel as if a critical mass was gathering. If I was going to be heard by the Mets, I knew I needed every last bit of support I could get. And this was crunch time.

I was winding up the Internet tour with seven different primaries, all hosted within a single week. I wanted to demonstrate widespread, simultaneous support—along with the ability to multitask—and I wanted to give the voters a chance at a virtual national primary. In presidential primaries, this is generally known as Super Tuesday. For me, in honor of the oversize former Mets slugger who ate himself out of the league, it would be Mo Vaughn Monday.

I spoke to Kerel Cooper of OnTheBlack.com via Skype video—and earned 80 percent of the vote on that site. My support topped 80 percent over at the Eddie Kranepool Society as well, where the incomparable Steve Keane graciously had me on his radio program. And the same thing happened everywhere else—at professor of literature at Hofstra University Dana Brand's Mets blog; at Brooklyn Mets Fan, where filmmaker Adam Salazar wrote about the Mets; at Section 518, where disgruntled fan JD chose not to publish his last name (he just wanted a place to write about the Mets, not to gain from it in any way); at My Summer Family, where Taryn Cooper blended astute fan observations with humor; and even at the national site Baseball Think Factory, where so many of my ideas about baseball had been peer reviewed.

Still, no call from the Wilpons. No indication that they'd even decided to change horses. At a press event in August, when Fred Wilpon was asked if Omar Minaya would be the general manager in 2011, his response was, "Is the sun going to come up tomorrow?" Either Fred Wilpon had advance notice on some truly catastrophic astronomical event, or he seemed to be saying that nothing would change next year for the New York Mets.

At some point, in the midst of all the voting, Rachel asked me exactly what it would mean if I did get the job as general manager.

"Well, you'd never see me. It's pretty much a constant job. And we'd have to make Mirabelle a really lifelike poster of me, so she'll remember who I am."

"What does the job pay?"

"Well, Omar Minaya gets one million dollars a year. So obviously if I get his contract, you can quit teaching if you want. But my guess is they'd start me with a lot less. And then, after the team takes off, a lot more."

The question never was, at any point, whether I would be up to the job. Of that I was certain: I could handle it. I'd simply spent too much time preparing, had an encyclopedic knowledge of precisely the things I needed to be on top of, and felt certain that I could put the time in and add skills as necessary should there be aspects to running a major-league ballclub I had somehow overlooked. I'd met so many of the people in these positions. And over and over again I'd been disappointed with their outlooks. Why were they all still adherents to wisdom that had been dismissed decades before? I knew I was inexperienced, but at the same time, here they were, spitting out the same banalities I'd heard from the media, the same ones I'd processed, dissected, and debunked time and again.

And what did these guys have on me? Experience, sure. They'd been around baseball, something that used to be regarded with a lot of respect. And yet those kinds of barriers had come down. I watched every game, every year. In my career as a sportswriter, I'd spent a lot of time in press conferences, locker rooms, dugouts. I had personal relationships with players. What more could being a "baseball man" really mean? Could I really look at myself in the mirror—could anyone look at me in any reflective surface—and say that I *wasn't* a baseball man?

My heroes, like Theo Epstein, had both the knowledge and the experience. But Epstein wasn't leaving Boston. And he, too, had once lacked experience—it didn't stop him from ending eighty-six years of futility. Meanwhile, it wasn't clear that the Mets had someone with the knowledge about how to fix the team, no matter the experience. So I was ready with that knowledge, and the day-and-night focus I gave to the team anyway. The experience would come.

August gave way to September. Rachel returned to work, and in addition to my responsibilities as a writer, I had now assumed daytime control over Mirabelle. I wrote furiously during her naps, but I wasn't content to let the television be a babysitter while she was awake. I remembered those Spanish lessons calling. I knew she'd be in preschool faster than the Mets could lose a no-hitter. I was determined to maximize my time with her. Some of it, we listened to great music—I'd pick an artist, tell her about Art Tatum or Ella Fitzgerald, then play her some songs. We spent a fair amount of time in front of a colorful map of the United States, going over things like the tight Senate and House races. And naturally, a large amount of our discussion took place in front of the twenty-four-by-thirty-six mock-up of Citi Field in our kitchen that served as a real-time organizational summary of the New York Mets.

Back in 2005, when Rachel was still getting the hang of the baseball obsession she'd inexplicably signed on for, discussion turned to the fact that she considered herself a visual learner.

To hear me discuss players was one thing, but to see it in front of her, well, that would give her access to my world. Looking back on it now, our first efforts were crude—a Wright Brothers aircraft compared to today's supersonic jets. Just a plain white twenty-four-by-thirty-six poster board with a crudely drawn baseball diamond, each player picture pasted on the paper, replacements added hastily on pink Post-its. Only a handful of prospects to be found in the minor-league system on the far right. The disabled list, drawn ludicrously small in the bottom left corner, reflected the optimism of March rather than the cruel reality of September. But it was a start.

Gradually, our creations became grander, a combination of my obsession and Rachel's remarkable organizational skills. For 2006, each player was mounted on a color-coded Post-it with name, uniform number, position, and lefty/righty designation. Each day, we changed the lineup to reflect the team the Mets would put on the field. In 2007 the disabled list expanded, symbolized by a red cross. The walls had always been marked with Shea Stadium's dimensions, but now we added the retired uniform numbers out in left field—14, 37, 41, and 42. Places were found for the manager, the coaching staff, the general manager. Rachel drew a tiny TV, where pictures of Gary Cohen, Keith Hernandez, and Ron Darling fit perfectly. By 2008, Ralph Kiner, the longtime broadcaster, had his own tab as well, as did field reporter Kevin Burkhardt. The minor-league system had nearly thirty players. The home run apple sat, optimistically aloft, in right-center field. And so Rachel would know who the Mets were playing, twenty-nine pennants (tabs cut into triangles) held logos for the twenty-nine other teams.

The charts were a source of amusement to our friends and family. And this wasn't your typical, beer-commercial split down the gender line. The men we knew thought we were crazy, too. But the chart had its desired effect. Rachel knew the Mets top to bottom. And I often found myself, when working on a story, in front of the chart—making sure whatever relatively small piece I was working on fit within the larger context of the team's future.

In 2009, we decided the chart needed to reflect our new surroundings more accurately. We were home owners; at the same time, the Mets had traded in their increasingly shabby Shea Stadium for the sparkling Citi Field. I found a high-resolution photo of Citi Field and we took it to Staples, got it laminated and mounted, and nailed it into our kitchen nook. No longer would the annual task be to reconstruct the Mets to reflect a winter of changes. Now the Mets would be updated year-round. The photo was perfect to incorporate every detail we'd had and more. We added Howie Rose and Wayne Hagin in the radio booth. Mr. Met, clearly an oversight, got his own tab (Position: Mascot). The minor leagues held the fifty Mets most likely to see action over the course of the season. The opposing team's pennant went in the visiting dugout. Beneath this behemoth, our cats ate and drank. I like to think they, too, gained greater insight into the totality of the New York Mets.

And so Mirabelle and I would often pass the time in front of that chart. I'd tell her a little about Kirk Nieuwenhuis, an outfield prospect, or give her the tortured injury history of John Maine. Whatever it was I'd said, it clearly had an effect. Mirabelle now sat for innings at a time, watching televised baseball with me. And in early September, Rachel and I picked out a four o'clock game against the Phillies with a temperature just right for a baby. My Mirabelle, just over five months old, watched a complete game, in person. A throwback baby, clearly, with no specialists required to finish what she started and no toys necessary to distract her. Only the occasional lift in the air so she could smile at the people behind us. Amazingly, even the Phillies fans smiled back at her, even though she wasn't a cheesesteak.

Eight days later, I gave my acceptance speech before a crowd of both my delegates and some ordinary Mets fans in the general parking lot at Citi Field. Once again, Rachel and Mirabelle joined me. Indeed, Rachel had become so accustomed to my crusade by this point that when I told her I'd be giving an acceptance speech for the pretend nomination, and gestured meaningfully at a just-purchased megaphone, her response was to simply write the date on the calendar. A supportive wife? Or had I utterly crushed her spirit? Only Rachel knows for sure.

Once again I was determined not to prepare a speech ahead of time—as ever I was certain that expressing, simply, how LOGIC, TRANSPARENCY, and PASSION would transform the New York Mets would win me all the support I could desire. Prior to the twelve-fifteen speech, I walked around the parking lot in my best suit and New York Mets lapel pin, inviting people to come over and join me. Some of them, naturally, assumed I was a vagrant and responded accordingly. (I was wearing my best suit, but . . . I'm a writer.) Still, folks joined the group waiting in front of the MEGDAL FOR GM banner we'd hung. And the majority of the conversations I had were, in fact, revelatory. I'd approached a group of three men, all in Met gear, in their thirties. I introduced myself and said that I was running for general manager of the New York Mets, and the most skeptical in the group said, "Well, why should I support you?"

I told him about my professional background and began to detail what I would do. He stopped me again and asked: "Well, who would you hire as manager?" I could have given him the popular answer—Bobby Valentine. But I didn't. I explained that I'd pick a manager based on his ability to communicate with players and make sound baseball decisions, and that I couldn't commit to that without extended conversations with various candidates. And I think that simple honesty, rather than a pat answer, intrigued all three of them. When I returned to the banner, they were waiting to hear me.

Sad to say, no one from the Mets had joined them. I'd kept Deep Swoboda aware of my primary victories and let him know that if the Mets had begun preliminary discussions about a new general manager, I'd be happy to come in and interview as soon as it made sense for the team. I'd sent Jeff Wilpon a letter that expanded on this idea as well.

Dear Mr. Wilpon,

As you may know, I have been running to become the next general manager of the New York Mets since the spring. I have covered the Mets for most of my adult life, having written on baseball for the *New York Times*, ESPN, SNY, MLBTradeRumors.com, and many other publications.

However, my qualifications for this position, knowledge and energy I would bring to the task, and comprehensive plan for LOGIC, TRANSPARENCY, and PASSION date back to my early childhood.

So while many people are calling for drastic and short-sighted changes to your baseball team, or ludicrously blaming you for, let's face it, spending tons of money and building an incomparable baseball stadium, I have studied the issues at hand for decades and believe you will embrace my comprehensive solutions. Your fan base already has: In eighteen separate primaries at Mets Web sites around the Internet, I averaged 74 percent in support of my campaign.

In other words, hire me, and it will not only profit the franchise for years to come, it will make you both heroes in the eyes of the fans and my colleagues in the press.

With the opportunity to serve as your general manager, I will bring about long-term prosperity in your team's on-field major-league success, make the farm system into a breeding ground for both talent and low-cost major-league solutions, and most important, make Citi Field a place that regularly sells out while turning your casual fans into regular customers.

I have been a fan since the age of six, a season ticket holder since moving to the area in 2006, and will root for the New York Mets long after my tenure as general manager ends. I am actively raising my five-month-old daughter as a Mets fan of similar intensity—so rest assured, the plan I wish to put into place has nothing to do with my short-term job security as GM, and everything to do with making your primary investment the success you both deserve.

Moreover, I want to watch October baseball with my father, who raised me on Brooklyn Dodgers stories, my wife, who is as dedicated to your franchise as I am by virtue of having to live with me, and my daughter, who should get the chance to regularly experience the joy I felt in 1986, and that my father felt in 1969 and 1955.

I ask that, before you make any decisions about who your

next general manager will be, you take some time and meet with me. I will happily come to the place of your choosing at your convenience. I am certain that, once I detail for you exactly how to turn the New York Mets into the consistent winner you both deserve and have sought during your tenure in ownership, we will find it mutually beneficial to work together.

Thank you for taking the time to hear me out. I look forward to hearing from you.

Sincerely,
Howard Megdal

Deep Swoboda had assured me that Jeff Wilpon received the letter and wished me luck with the acceptance speech. So really it was up to the Mets to make the next move.

Meanwhile, I began my public address. I thanked the assembled group, the delegates who couldn't make it as well, and spoke frankly about the changes I believed the Mets needed to make. I'd tackled second base and begun to untangle the outfield when a group of three security officers drove up in a golf cart and demanded that we stop. I calmly told the most aggressive of the three, a man who repeatedly blocked my cousin/videographer from continuing to accumulate footage, that I had let the Mets know I'd be giving this speech. Astoundingly, he was displaying the same kind of behavior so many Mets fans had experienced: creating an atmosphere where we were warily tolerated instead of welcomed. Back in the corner of a mostly empty lot—after all, crowds that small don't need very many cars—we were making less of a fuss than virtually any typical tailgate, complete as they usually are with a loud radio and spirited games of catch or Wiffle ball. After the third remonstration by the security bully, ignoring that I'd told him the Mets knew of my speech (and frankly I was pretty sure I had a right to stand in the parking spot I'd paid for and talk, regardless), he finally decided to make some mysterious call on his walkie-talkie. After another five minutes or so, he made his grand proclamation: We were allowed to continue, but the banner had to come down. Since my primary goal was to communicate, I acquiesced. With that, he and his two assistants were on their way, presumably in search of some other fans to harass.

The man who'd grilled me about who the Mets should hire as manager spoke up. "I'm sorry, but I just have to say, That wasn't right. Here you are, trying to talk about how you want to make the New York Mets better. You're actually here, unlike a lot of Mets fans. And they treat you like you're a criminal."

And it was hard to fathom on some level: I'd put so much time and energy into the proper ways to make the New York Mets better—something that would emotionally benefit me, to be sure, but an improvement that would make life much better, professionally and financially, for the stakeholders in the team. And all I got was some petty harassment for my troubles. At the same time, I knew the Mets couldn't publicly endorse someone who was making the public case that the way they conducted business needed to change. At long last, I needed to trust that my message would change fifty years of culture, whether or not the Mets embraced me as the messenger that the fans had.

I assured the man that this security guard had been acting on his own. But I also reiterated that if I received the opportunity to become the general manager, part of changing the culture of the team would mean making sure that every employee of the New York Mets understood that it was the fans who made their jobs possible. Simply put, cut attendance in half and half as many security guards are needed. You need to make sure the drunk people fighting get separated? Fine. But the group of Mets fans politely assembled and talking about the team, with the Mets notified? The only threat any of us posed was the possibility we'd be alienated enough not to return. I knew I'd never be one of those alienated. But I couldn't speak for everyone, and the attendance figures clearly showed that the Mets hadn't developed much goodwill among their customers to weather losing seasons.

When my speech concluded—on my own terms this time— the man who'd once been a skeptic asked me to write the name of my campaign Web site down so he'd be able to read more about the effort and how he could help. The encounter left me feeling ambivalent. Obviously, it was exciting that my message had affected him so intensely. But I also realized that for many Mets fans, the Mets exist outside of the blogosphere. There were hundreds of thousands of Mets fans I didn't meet and explain the principles of LOGIC, TRANSPARENCY, and PASSION to, people who simply loved their baseball team but weren't steeped in the daily cycle of information about the New York Mets. To really capture a fan movement in full, I explained to Rachel, I would have needed to go to that Citi Field parking lot before every home game, to public events all over the tri-state area, to rotary clubs, youth groups, and parades. In other words: I should have run the way a person runs for president.

"And imagine how much we'd have seen you then," Rachel replied.

It was true. I wanted the Mets to be great for my family. I didn't want the Mets to be great more than I wanted time with my family. Oh, I'd serve as general manager if that's what it took to put the Mets on track. But I realized, sitting there in Citi Field with Rachel, Mirabelle, and a number of delegates, that what I really wanted was a Theo Epstein to take control of my New York Mets the way he'd saved Kostya's Boston Red Sox. If anything, becoming general manager, with all of the inherent late nights and weeks away from my family, would be at cross purposes with what I wanted most, which was to enjoy baseball with my family. I didn't want to Skype Rachel and Mirabelle to tell them about the latest trade; I wanted to race over to Citi Field with them the day after a sage general manager made a fantastic trade and watch the newest Met lead the team to victory. And I wanted the chance to interview that player, put his acquisition in perspective, and tell the fans why I thought it mattered so much. But then . . . I wanted to go home.

That afternoon, Mirabelle went a solid seven-plus, drifting off in my lap near the bottom of the eighth inning. The Mets lost, as I knew they eventually would with Mirabelle present. Still, she ended the year 2–1, which is a solid rookie fan performance. We bundled her up, careful to protect her from the surprisingly potent September sun, and walked out of Citi Field for the last time as a family in 2010. I thought about how often we'd left a Mets game stung by defeat—so often against the Phillies, or following Game 7 of the 2006 NLCS, or on the final days of the 2007 and 2008 seasons. (For the 2008 finale, Rachel actually stayed home to help prepare Rosh Hashanah dinner, so I only got to hear secondhand about her angry meltdown when Jerry Manuel left Scott Schoeneweis, a lefty specialist, in against a right-handed power hitter.) Would this be the pattern Mirabelle would experience as well? Or were there memories like the ones I'd had in 1999, 2000, and even 2006 in store for her? Or better?

As we sat in stalled traffic on the Whitestone Expressway, Rachel and I discussed the people we'd met, how much we liked my delegates (many of whom were, or had become, friends), and started planning our annual trip to Port St. Lucie in the spring. It was the ultimate work/pleasure trip, and, for the first time, it would include Mirabelle. Then Rachel asked: "So with the GM job, what comes next?" "I don't know," I said to Rachel. "I just hope the Mets are ready for a change."

Chapter 16

WHEN IT WAS GOOD

A S MY SUMMER-LONG campaign began to stretch into the fall and I began to feel the job slipping away from me, I tried to remember what it had been all about in the first place. As a fan, I'd spent the last few years being angry, waiting for something to happen, something to change my fortunes. As a writer, I had a chance to experience these missteps up close. But with reality setting in—the Mets were going to make a change, but it probably didn't involve hiring me—I felt something un-expected. I felt hopeful. And that made it easy to remember a time, not so long ago, when rooting for the Mets meant feeling hopeful, too.

When you spend so much time imagining what an event will be like, the moment itself always seems surreal: Our dreams are predicated on the notion that they aren't going to happen. Maybe that's why, when my father and I drove from South Jersey to Game 4 of the 1999 National League Championship Series, I kept expecting to wake up. I'd watched Todd Pratt homer just over the outstretched arm of Steve Finley on Saturday afternoon in the TV room at Bard. That night I packed and drove the three hours to Cherry Hill. I knew I'd be watching the NLCS with my father, even before we went to Shea for Game 4.

What followed, at first . . . wasn't pretty. We watched the Braves take Game 1, 4–2, but that came as no surprise—Atlanta had Greg Maddux on the mound, their Rolls-Royce, while the Mets threw Masato Yoshii, the Ford Escort of pitchers. Game 2 went Atlanta's way as well, 4–3, with Kevin Millwood outpitching Kenny Rogers. The Braves actually used the detested John Rocker as a setup man and let John Smoltz earn the save by throwing a scoreless ninth on his throw day. As usual, Bobby Cox seemed to take pleasure in parading his impressive pitching talent in front of the Mets. Every call to the bullpen felt like piling on. Al Leiter was fierce in Game 3, allowing only a run on a Mike Piazza error in the first inning. But future Met Tom Glavine was even stingier, pitching seven shutout innings. John Franco and Armando Benitez held the Braves in the eighth and ninth, but the Mets went quietly to Rocker—again—and lost, 1–0. The Braves were hardly dominating—they'd won three games by a total of four runs—but the Mets trailed, 3–0, in a best-of-seven series. This being the old millennium, no team had ever come back from 3–0 to win a series.

The Shea crowd had a spirited feel as we walked to our seats prior to Game 4. But I couldn't help also noticing that some fans were worrying: "I can't believe we bought playoff tickets to watch the Braves sweep us at home!"

Smoltz, the Game 2 closer, pitched for Atlanta, squaring off against Rick Reed, our solid number-two starter. And just as with the Red Sox five years later against the Yankees, everyone knew that the Mets were one mistake away from seeing their archrivals win—and on their home field. My father and I were stationed way up in the right-field stands, just in fair territory at Shea Stadium. One couldn't call the seats terrific, but it seemed right that for a playoff game at Shea Stadium, we wouldn't sit in our typical baseball seats—both father and son preferred the first-base line, between home and first. Though the game moved quickly, due to the absence of runs or walks— neither pitcher allowed a free pass—the tension kept me from thinking about how fast my first playoff game at Shea seemed to be disappearing. In the bottom of the sixth, John Olerud blasted a home run to right field, giving the Mets a 1–0 lead. But the applause was quickly replaced by more anticipation. These were the Braves, and it was only a matter of time before they struck back.

In the top of the eighth inning, with Rick Reed pitching a one-hit shutout, they did just that. Brian Jordan homered to left-center on the very first pitch of the inning, and Ryan Klesko followed with a shot to right just two pitches later. It felt like lightning had struck—once, and then again seconds later. Just like that, the Mets were six outs away from elimination. I checked to see if my hair was singed.

Roger Cedeno led off the bottom of the eighth with a single. Rey Ordonez, who never learned to bunt despite an astonishing inability to hit, then popped up a sacrifice attempt to the first baseman. After Benny Agbayani struck out, the Mets were four outs from elimination. Cedeno stole second, however, and pinch hitter Melvin Mora drew a two-out walk. That's when Bobby Cox decided to crush the Mets once and for all, bringing in John Rocker for the four-out save.

This was before the public had read Rocker's notorious comments about the 7 train: "[It looks] like you're riding through Beirut next to some kid with purple hair, next to some queer with AIDS, right next to some dude who just got out of jail for the fourth time, right next to some 20-year-old mom with four kids." This, about the subway ride I'd dreamed of my whole childhood, about the city, the people, and the team I loved. I had no idea at that moment just how much I would come to hate John Rocker. But I did know that he was a physically scary, dominating closer for the team that ran over my Mets year after year.

It seemed as though my team had spent the entire decade trailing the Braves. As the Mets struggled through losing seasons throughout much of the nineties, the Braves just kept winning division titles. They just always seemed to win, usually beating the Mets in the process, even when they didn't need to. Going into the final weekend of the 1998 season, Atlanta had already clinched a playoff spot. The Mets needed, it turned out, just one win to keep their season alive. And the Braves crushed them—swept the series—and it wasn't particularly close. Bobby Cox even started Greg Maddux in the season finale, letting him go six innings in a meaningless game when he could have been resting his ace for the playoffs. That's how much Bobby Cox enjoyed beating the Mets.

So it seemed inevitable to me that Rocker would take care of business. Facing his first hitter, John Olerud, Rocker already had a big advantage—he was left-handed, pitching to another lefty. And then Bobby Valentine sent Mora and Cedeno on a daring double steal. It was precisely the type of move Bobby Cox usually made. It caught Atlanta off guard and put the go-ahead run into scoring position. It sent a message: We're not afraid of you. We're finished playing timid. A few pitches later, the consummate hitter Olerud managed to sneak a single through a drawn-in infield into center field. Mora and Cedeno scored. Pandemonium reigned.

I remember turning to my father and saying, "This is why we came here."

In many ways, that 1999 series was a premonition of the larger miracle to come for the 2004 Red Sox. The Mets were four outs, instead of three, from elimination. The game turned on a stolen base and a single, and suddenly the favorite team was back on its heels. But for the moment, the stakes were far lower for the two of us. We drove home, stopping for a late-night snack at New Jersey's best diner, Mastoris. And being baseball fans, we calculated exactly how the Mets could come back and win the series, improbable as it might be. Sure, Masato Yoshii faced Greg Maddux again—but Yoshii wasn't terrible, and maybe the Mets could keep it close and win late. As it turned out, of course, what followed that Sunday afternoon into evening was perhaps the greatest game in Mets history, certainly the greatest outside of 1986. Fifteen innings, another comeback just two outs from elimination this time, five hours and forty-six minutes of pulsating drama. This one I watched with my father in Cherry Hill. And it was unforgettable. I could still feel the Shea chill and the sounds of thousands chanting, "Let's go Mets!" which would get inside of you as you traveled down the exit ramps following an epic Mets victory.

The battle of Game 6, played back in Atlanta, was ultimately a disappointment. Though the Mets stormed back from a 5–0 deficit, even taking leads in the eighth and tenth innings, the Braves erased them each time and advanced to the World Series on a bases-loaded walk issued by Kenny Rogers. I'd returned to Bard by then, and I remembered walking the campus late into the night, stunned that the season had ended in such a sudden way. Normally, the Mets gave you ample time to plan for the end—months, usually, to get your emotional affairs in order—so by the time the opponent is issuing the last rites, you've already cobbled together the small rites that kept you going until pitchers and catchers reported. Not this year.

Still, a season like that, one that ended just two games shy of the World Series, didn't leave me angry. Like most Mets fans, I'd simply marveled at the reality that when all the other regular-season teams had exited the stage, the baseball world had turned its eyes toward the Mets—our Mets—and Shea Stadium, once again, served as its center.

That winter, I discovered what the Internet could do for an off-season. Suddenly, even the dormant Mets were a 24-7 obsession, the kind previously reserved for the regular season. And though the 2000 season had the same unhappy ending— this time at the hands of the Yankees—it was impossible to feel cheated.

This time, what I hoped was becoming an annual tradition— the relentless working of the phone to secure playoff tickets— landed me a pair of obstructed-view seats, loge level, along the third-base line. The obstruction was, in the scheme of things, relatively unobtrusive—an overhang made it difficult to see balls high in the air. Our section moved like synchronized swimmers, dipping our heads down to track the pop-ups and high flies, then gradually rising to full height again as the ball fell harmlessly into a fielder's mitt.

Long before we knew the game would be known as the Bobby Jones One-Hitter, the experience had particular meaning for my father and me. He'd taken the train up from South Jersey, meeting me in Penn Station. We took the 7 train for the first time together. And riding the 7 train that year, after John Rocker's comments, felt like a badge of honor. We loved the city defiantly (even if, technically, it wasn't our city), making a note to enjoy the cultural diversity that made up the New York Mets' fan base. We held ourselves, righteously, above Braves fans, who couldn't be bothered to fill their own stadium during the playoffs.

The day was a bit overcast and a bit windy, feeling very much like what I thought of as "college-football weather." Thinking about it a little more, I realized this was what Billy Crystal described, based on his childhood, as "World Series weather." There was an important lesson here: If you grew up a Yankees fan in the 1950s, October 8 was World Series time. If you grew up a Mets fan in the 1990s, October 8 was well into the off-season.

The Mets entered the game with a 2–1 series lead over the San Francisco Giants, needing just one win to clinch the best-of-five NLDS. After the Giants took the opener at home, 5–1, each of the next two games had been riveting baseball. In Game 2, also in San Francisco, the Mets staked Al Leiter to a 4–1 lead. But closer Armando Benitez, in one of many instances of blowing up in huge spots, allowed a game-tying three-run homer to J. T. Snow in the bottom of the ninth. No matter; in the top of the tenth, Jay Payton hit a go-ahead single to center, and John Franco closed out the game by striking out Barry Bonds, looking, on a changeup.

The two teams flew east to play Saturday's Game 3 at Shea Stadium. I'd stayed at school a day into fall break, knowing I'd be back at Shea myself on Sunday to see the game with my father. So, alone in my room, I watched Russ Ortiz, Rick Reed, and the two bullpens battle into the thirteenth inning, when finally, the Triple-A hitter himself, Benny Agbayani, slugged a game-winning home run into the left-field porch. I called home immediately to let my parents know I was driving down—a CD filled with Mets highlights and songs already prepared as my accompaniment—and my father answered not with "Hello" but with "That is some Triple-A hitter."

Now my father and I had the chance to see something more exciting than the Mets avoiding a sweep: If everything went right on that blustery Sunday, we'd see the Mets clinch a spot in the NLCS. And other motivating factors existed as well. Barry Bonds, for example. I don't mean to brag, but I have always considered myself a leader of men when it comes to not liking Barry Bonds. Yes, legions of people would boo him as he shattered record after hallowed record, holding up signs with steroid needles and asterisks and Lord knew what else. But Bonds and I had an older feud. He'd helped to crush my 1990 Mets, who finished second to his Pirates, and for a decade since, he'd been one of the best players in baseball but always seemed so mirthless doing it—as if he was only allowing us to see his unparalleled gifts because there was a lot of money in it for him.

The Mets' starter, Bobby Jones, had longtime emotional ties to me, too—as he probably did to everyone in the stands that day. Thanks to superior command, he'd somehow managed to become a top pitching prospect without much in the way of raw stuff. So no one expected much from him—but he managed to lead many of the lesser Met staffs of the early-to-mid nineties. He finished eighth in the Rookie of the Year voting in 1994, behind such stalwarts as John Hudek, William VanLandingham, and Hector Carrasco. He made the All-Star team in 1997, won 15 games, and even pitched a scoreless inning in that midsummer classic. Generally, he gave the Mets 30 starts, wrangled a league-average ERA, and stayed healthy and consistent. But in 2000, finally blessed with a strong team around him, he appeared to be disintegrating. In three starts, he failed to last beyond the fourth inning—in the third start, he failed to record an out. Bogged down with an unsightly 16.20 ERA, Jones went to Triple-A at age thirty to try and find his form. And he did, to an extent—a month later he returned and posted a 4.56 ERA over the rest of the season. Still, it was generally understood that Jones didn't have a role on future Met teams. We knew this might be his last moment of glory with the Mets.

But that is one of the beauties of baseball—anything is possible. Jones, who'd made a career of being ordinary, absolutely dominated the Giants. And being Jones, he dominated softly. He struck out just five. He allowed a couple of walks and a lone hit. When Robin Ventura homered in the top of the first, Jones had all the run support he'd need. Shea Stadium, it has been written, shook when witnessing its greatest moments. I remember that feeling of uneasy excitement as Jones faced his final batter of the afternoon: Barry Bonds. And as the routine fly ball settled back into our view and, shortly thereafter, center fielder Jay Payton's glove, I hugged my father. We and fifty-five thousand other Mets fans jumped up and down like little children. I have highlights of the 2000 season on my iPod still; when the final out of the Bobby Jones game plays, I tear up every time.

The Mets took care of St. Louis in the NLCS, and though it bothered me that they wouldn't get another crack at the Braves, the reality of the 2000 Subway Series was almost more than I could believe. In retrospect, again, it was clear the Mets simply didn't have the talent of their Bronx rivals. And maybe that's what made the endless walk around the Bard campus bearable after seeing Mike Piazza's fly ball fall just short of tying up Game 5, and Derek Jeter celebrating on the Shea Stadium infield. Losing to the Yankees was a bitter pill to swallow. But it was infinitely better than a season that could have ended a month earlier.

It would be another six years until I experienced postseason baseball again. Much had happened in the intervening period. Now I lived within easy driving distance of Shea Stadium. I was married and could afford a partial-season ticket plan that gave me the option to buy postseason tickets. My years of redialing were over, not least because the Mets no longer sold playoff tickets that way—it all happened over the Internet now. And the heroes of those postseason runs back in 1999 and 2000 were long since purged from the roster—a consequence of Steve Phillips's life-begins-at-thirty approach to building a team.

When I revisit the postseason memories of 2006, I actually begin in September. Rachel and I drove to Cherry Hill so we could watch the Mets clinch the National League East on television with my parents. The Mets needed just one win against the hapless Pirates in Pittsburgh to officially become NL East champions for the first time in eighteen years. The four of us piled onto the couch in my parents' basement—the best viewing place for my then-fancy video feed from MLB.tv. On an occasionally jumpy video, we watched the Mets drop three straight games. The losses were not cause for worry—the Mets still led the division by thirteen and a half games. All it meant was that they'd clinch at home, an echo of 1986, when they'd lost to the Phillies with me in attendance, only to clinch at Shea. This was cosmic retribution—I'd get to see them clinch after all.

I quickly bought up eight tickets from Mets.com in Section 1, upper reserved, behind home plate, and invited all comers to join Rachel and me for history. (My father actually begged off—he'd save his sleepless-night trips to New York for the playoffs.) I remember spending much of that Monday night trying to explain to Rachel why I was so excited about something that had been a fait accompli for most of the summer. There was something about the officialness of it. No one could take it away. The Braves had been division champions every year from the time before my voice changed until the year I got engaged. But that reign was over. A similar feeling of ecstasy engulfed the crowd. I told Rachel, "This year is finally the year." I was incapable of believing anything else.

After cheering for another five minutes, ten minutes, fifteen minutes, we finally left our seats. In the tight corridors outside of the upper reserved seating, concession stands were doing a booming business. I purchased a 2006 NL East Champions shirt—obviously. It was complete with the numbers and names of every Met on the roster. You'll never be forgotten, Mike DeFelice, even though each time I wash the shirt you fade just a little.

And yes, the 2006 Mets came up short in pursuit of a championship as well. But the longer I've been around, the more distance I get from that incredible '86 team, the more I realize how thrilling it is just to be a part of the hunt. Sitting in the mezzanine for Game 1 of the NLDS, I saw a young John Maine keep the Mets in the game, saw Carlos Delgado launch a long home run, and celebrated a Mets victory with Rachel and my father. Already the partial-season plan had been worth it. The plan also allowed us to purchase NLCS tickets to Game 1 and Game 6, both Mets wins. I'd now attended five home playoff games for the Mets in seven years, and the Mets were 5–0. You can be sure this was on my mind when the opportunity arose, on the day of Game 7, to attend. I remember calling Rachel from work and explaining: We had no choice. We'd been up until around one thirty the night before at Game 6; she was utterly exhausted. But she also knew how rarely Mets fans, or any baseball fans (except for Yankees fans), got to see their team play for a chance to go to the World Series. There wasn't a chance that either of us would miss it.

Our seats, courtesy of one of Rachel's relatives, were in the upper reaches of the left-field stands. That meant we had a relatively good view of everything except plays made near the left-field wall. What this meant, specifically, was a unique experience of one of the most dramatic moments in Mets history. Endy Chavez's leaping, running, impossible catch that kept the game knotted at 1–1 in the sixth inning looked like this: a towering fly ball, clearly trouble; a left fielder with his head down, sprinting away from home plate; then, as they both vanished from my view, silence, followed by a roar that drowned out anything I'd ever heard at Shea Stadium. What felt like an omen of ultimate success turned out to be the last time I'd hear Mets fans react like that. I recently asked Rachel if she could believe how long it had been since Mets fans were happy, and she told me, "I don't really remember what that feels like."

But as we left Shea Stadium after Carlos Beltran made the game's final out, even while Rachel was crying, I felt okay. This had nothing to do with some kind of macho front—I'm not terribly convincing at that anyway—and more to do with the feeling that the situation just wasn't that grim. "Think about how much extra baseball we got this year," I said to console Rachel. "Think about all the times we saw Jose Reyes hit a triple. This was a great year."

And I think, for the most part, all Mets fans want is that feeling—not a championship passed down as if it was their birthright, the way the Yankees faithful seem to, but, simply put, a chance. No fan has a right to expect titles, and the mere act of doing so takes away the thrill. When John Olerud singled off John Rocker, fifty-five thousand fans didn't sigh with relief over the expected coming to pass. Bobby Jones didn't merely fulfill the terms of his social contract with Mets fans by coming up big in October. When Paul Lo Duca tagged out a pair of Dodgers at home on the same play in Game 1 of the 2006 NLDS, no Mets fan laughed knowingly simply because other teams exist merely to be defeated come October.

It was memories like those that felt ripped from me when I look at my still-unused tickets to 2007 and 2008 playoff games that the Mets, thanks to late-September swoons, never played. It's moments like those that effective management of the team can make possible. No GM can guarantee those moments will always turn out well. And no fan, being truly honest with himself, wants that guarantee, either. That's what makes it good.

Chapter 17

DEUS EX ALDERSON

I'D SPOKEN WITH Deep Swoboda after my acceptance speech, and he assured me that the Mets would be in touch once a decision had been made about how to proceed on the general manager front. Until then, I was left to follow that process, like everyone else, through the press. I chose not to put questions about the future to Jerry Manuel; the last few times I'd seen him, at postgame press conferences, he already looked like a man who knew the execution was nigh. You don't ask a prisoner about electrocution during his last meal.

But as September turned to October, the rumored front-office names had a very different sound to them. From the moment Frank Cashen stepped down as general manager in 1991 through Omar Minaya's tenure, each man who ran the Mets had spent significant time within the organization—one reason, I felt sure, why so many of them made the same mistakes. Not since Cashen back in 1980 had the Mets stepped outside the comfort zone of their own people to find a new leader.

On the final Friday of the season, SI.com's Jon Heyman had the scoop: Neither Omar Minaya nor Jerry Manuel would return. And a most intriguing paragraph, buried deep in the story, kept me buzzing to Rachel all weekend: "The Mets are planning to go outside the organization for the GM position and are thought to be considering several people, including former Diamondbacks GM Josh Byrnes, White Sox assistant GM Rick Hahn and former A's GM Sandy Alderson."

Each of these three potential candidates represented a completely different take on running a baseball team from the current Mets regime. Hahn was the well-respected numbers guy for White Sox GM Kenny Williams. Josh Byrnes had been fired by a seemingly incompetent ownership group in Arizona and was a disciple of Theo Epstein. And Sandy Alderson—well, Sandy Alderson was the gateway for Bill James's work into mainstream baseball. Without Sandy Alderson, there's no Billy Beane, no *Moneyball*, no Theo Epstein.

Alderson's story was atypical. He'd served as a marine in Vietnam, then returned home to earn a law degree from Harvard. At that point, he discovered he had absolutely no taste for practicing law. He did, however, love baseball, and parlayed his work as general counsel for the Oakland Athletics into a job as general manager of the team at the tender age of thirty-six. Soon enough, the Athletics became regular contenders, with a farm system on par with the Cashen Mets. The A's won American League pennants each season from 1988 to 1990 and a World Series in 1989. During a period when Bill James was dismissed as a kook by many old-school baseball men, Alderson devoured his work and integrated many of his conclusions into the way he ran his baseball team. And he also was responsible for bringing a trio of front-office stars—Billy Beane, J.P. Ricciardi, and Paul DePodesta—to Oakland. Eventually, Michael Lewis wrote *Moneyball* about all three, each mentored by Sandy Alderson.

Ever since he'd left Oakland in 1997, he'd become a wandering success story. Tasked with improving the San Diego Padres, he'd helped the team capture back-to-back NL West titles as team president. Sent down to oversee baseball in the Dominican Republic, he drew rave reviews in helping to root out corruption in the process of selecting amateur baseball players. He spoke like . . . like the anti–Omar Minaya. The logic of the Harvard-trained lawyer was apparent in every sentence uttered and every move made. He seldom hid behind double-speak, bluntly telling reporters what was on his mind. And he dove into each task with the purpose of a marine.

LOGIC. TRANSPARENCY. PASSION. Alderson would be all three.

On October 7, the news broke that the Mets were seriously considering Alderson for their open GM spot. I'd also received a call from Deep Swoboda. I returned it, not knowing what to expect. We exchanged pleasantries, and then he turned unusually circumspect.

"We know that you've worked hard running for GM, and that certainly hasn't escaped the notice of anyone here. But I hope you can understand—the team is looking for someone with past experience in baseball, and while you've written about it, you don't have any time even in a front office . . ."

Deep Swoboda was a mensch. He was making what should have been an obvious point—the Mets preferred to go with the GM who'd won many championships while fundamentally changing the way front offices operated, rather than some guy running for the position online. The Mets were after something big, a fundamental change in the way they did business. Huge, landscape-altering changes were afoot, and it would take someone who'd been through it before to lead them to a better, safer place. While I knew that my skills and knowledge would translate to a better ballclub, it was impossible for the Wilpons to know that, even if I impressed them in an interview. And for all my confidence, I understood that hiring me to run the show, without any track record in a baseball front office, would be taking a chance.

In the meantime, Deep Swoboda didn't want to hurt my feelings. And why? It couldn't have been fear of screaming headlines in the New York tabloids: METS CHOOSE ALL-TIME GREAT GM OVER TOTAL UNKNOWN wouldn't exactly hurt the team's perception. Maybe he thought I'd really been certain that I'd be named GM, rather than understanding the long-shot nature of my campaign. Maybe he thought I was insane and treated me as one would treat a mental patient with a fragile equilibrium. Whatever the reason, it was an act of kindness, and I didn't want him to think it went unnoticed.

So I did my best to assure him that I certainly understood the Wilpons' desire for someone with experience. "I'd have loved the opportunity," I told him. "But now I'm just hoping for someone who will get the Mets back to October—for both my columns and my daughter." Deep Swoboda told me the Mets would have someone in place by the World Series. And they did.

But as the process unfolded, something new happened: The Mets gave out regular updates, not in sometimes contradictory leaks to the press, but in frequent e-mails from Jeff Wilpon. He e-mailed fans on October 4 to let them know why he was firing Jerry Manuel and Omar Minaya. He e-mailed them on October 15 to summarize the first round of interviews and to provide a timetable for the new GM hire. He provided another update on October 21, and named the final two candidates in still another e-mail the very next day. And a week later, on October 29, Wilpon sent his fifth e-mail update of the month to fans to announce that Sandy Alderson would be the twelfth general manager in team history. It was TRANSPARENCY unlike any I'd seen in my life as a Mets fan, let alone in the years I'd written about the team.

Story time changed for Mirabelle. Now it was time for her to learn about Alderson's tenure with the Oakland Athletics. I told her about 20-game winners picked off the scrap heap, draft hauls filled with three straight Rookies of the Year, and how he'd been involved with five Rickey Henderson transactions— always getting more when he traded him than what he'd give up to get him back.

Once the news broke that Alderson would be hired on October 27, I had three immediate tasks. One was to analyze the move for a number of editors who requested stories. Another was to write a concession speech; no candidate has ever been happier to yield the floor. And I needed to save some time to watch the final few innings of the 1986 World Series with Mirabelle. I'd made a point to do so every year on the anniversary of the team's last world championship. This time, Mirabelle would be joining me.

My concession speech, punctuated with a favorite picture of Mirabelle holding a large, soft rattle shaped like a baseball with METS written between its seams, read as follows:

With the announcement by the Mets that Sandy Alderson has been named the new general manager, we now know for certain that the Wilpons have heeded our call for LOGIC, TRANSPARENCY, and PASSION. As someone who writes about the Mets for a living, this development is encouraging for one who wishes to cover many postseason games. As someone who has loved the New York Mets since age six, the idea that I'll share those postseason memories with my baby daughter, wife, parents, and friends excites me beyond description.

Therefore, I am ending my campaign for general manager of the New York Mets, and enthusiastically endorsing Sandy Alderson. It is a choice that should thrill everyone who bleeds orange and blue, regardless of race, creed, or position on bunting. The sabermetrically inclined Mets fan and the student of baseball history will love this pick today. The fan who hungers for greater interaction and accountability from the front office will love this pick tomorrow. And it is easy to imagine a day, someday soon, when the results-only fan will celebrate with the rest of us on an October night at Citi Field. It has been Jon Niese since the Mets won a world championship, but tonight it is easy to imagine a winner before Niese is even arbitration-eligible.

I must thank the thousands of you who voted for me at eighteen Mets blogs throughout the blogosphere. It has been more rewarding than you can possibly know that so many of you expressed faith in my vision. Receiving 65 percent of the vote at Amazin' Avenue, where I have spent years as Poet Laureate, was gratifying, to be sure. To see those vote totals steadily increase as my campaign gained traction was humbling, culminating with 88 percent support at the Happy Recap. I want to thank all of my pledged delegates from those eighteen Mets blogs, from Mike Silva to Dana Brand, Toby Hyde to Zoë Rice, Greg Prince to Steve Keane, Dan Szymborski to Anthony DeRosa, Caryn Rose to Kerel Cooper, Adam Salazar to Matthew Artus, Eric Simon to

Shannon Shark, Taryn Cooper to JD. And to those who reached out to me personally to support the campaign, to the woman in North Carolina who bought a Megdal for GM bumper sticker, to the man who began a Megdal for GM Facebook group, and so many others, I am honored to have been your vehicle to demand better of the baseball team that binds us.

Together, when we began this campaign back in June, there were those who believed the status quo was sufficient, or that change of the magnitude we envisioned simply wasn't possible. Tonight, those cynics have been proven wrong. We now know that the arc of Mets history may be long, but it bends toward Alderson. Consider that the Mets have hired a general manager who embraced the work of Bill James and mentored Billy Beane. The Mets have hired a man who values process, rejects small sample sizes, and evaluates baseball players and transactions through the long-term goals of the franchises he runs.

The new general manager has been quoted as saying, "I really believe in as much interface with the public as possible." And oh, by the way? He said it to a blogger, during a comprehensive three-part interview.

And Sandy Alderson, at age sixty-two, has accomplished everything an executive can in Major League Baseball, yet has chosen to accept a position that will require massive amounts of his energy and time.

LOGIC. TRANSPARENCY. PASSION.

As a professional observer, I am impressed. As a fan, I am overjoyed. As a man moved to run for the position of general manager, despite it not being an elected position, the ascension of Sandy Alderson offers all the possibilities our campaign believed in without forcing me to spend long hours with Dayton Moore convincing him to sell low on Alex Gordon.

Most important, I want to thank my wife. When this campaign began at the Marriott Marquis on a rainy summer morning, she made certain my Mets lapel pin stayed on straight. When I told her of my plan to give a nomination acceptance speech at Citi Field, her response was to write it on the calendar. Only later did she request that I not get us thrown in jail. She has been a constant support, a sounding board for so many ideas, the person I sit with at Mets games I cover once the pregame work is finished and the person I drive home with once the postgame interviews are complete.

I want to thank my father, who gave me the gift of baseball, and my mother, who let me stay up with my father to watch Game 7 of the 1986 World Series. And I want to thank my baby daughter, who turns a lucky seven months old tomorrow, the day the Mets introduce Sandy Alderson. Like Alderson, she has a winning track record: The Mets are 2–1 in games she's attended. I wish nothing but success for them both. Thank you, and may God bless the New York Mets. He's blessed the Yankees long enough.

On Friday, October 29, Sandy Alderson was officially introduced as the next general manager of the New York Mets. Mirabelle and I watched on television from my office as, question by question, Alderson seemed ready to roll back a franchise-long penchant for easily avoidable mistakes. Later that night, poor Rachel, at the end of a long school week, got to hear each answer when I played her the recorded press conference, followed by Alderson's interview with Kevin Burkhardt. It was like a checklist of my deepest desires for the team or, put another way, my entire campaign platform. Alderson praised statistical information but made it clear he valued scouting information as well. He repeatedly spoke about the need to build up the farm system, elaborating in great detail about the dangers in long-term contracts—particularly, as he put it, "second-generation" contracts, precisely the kind of deals the Mets made so frequently. The Jason Bays, Mo Vaughns, Bobby Bonillas—these were all second-generation, long-term contracts. He emphasized the need not to rush prospects through the farm system, but rather to let them develop properly.

"If you think about how a team evolves, homegrown players are important, not just from a financial standpoint but from a fan standpoint," Alderson said.

He didn't promise championships, but said that given the resources available to the New York Mets, annual contention should be an attainable goal. He used the word *sustainable* twice. He spoke repeatedly of probabilities of success, and putting the team in the best possible position to succeed. And he reminded everyone repeatedly: This is all supposed to be fun. Then he answered fan questions solicited on Twitter.

The following few days will play in my memory for as long as I think about them, like a Hollywood montage in which the ingenue gets whisked off to a series of glamorous nightspots. There I am, looking up in awe, with triumphant music playing and headlines reading METS SET TO TALK TO DEPODESTA and RICCIARDI TO INTERVIEW WITH METS above my head. Soon enough, the Mets had hired the two men who, with Billy Beane, had formed the center of *Moneyball*'s Oakland Athletics. Both of them, in interviews with reporters, said that when Alderson called, they couldn't say no. Ricciardi had actually worked one day for Theo Epstein in Boston when Alderson called; he chose to come to New York instead.

Simply by hiring Sandy Alderson, the Mets made themselves a destination preferred over Theo Epstein's Red Sox. That's what I meant throughout the campaign when I talked about how quickly perceptions can change with the right leadership.

That weekend, Mirabelle's first Halloween, I elected to dress in costume as well. This year I went as Oliver Perez. I still had the jersey from when I'd been optimistic that he could become the pitcher his raw talent indicated he should be. When anyone asked who I was, I responded in as spooky a voice as I could muster, "I am the Ghost of Contracts Past!" I even told Rachel I would refuse assignment to the minor leagues, even if it cost me candy. Somehow that request didn't come up.

As the Alderson Era began in November, new developments seemed to buoy my spirits daily. Team executive vice president David Howard held a conference call with a number of bloggers, each of them a delegate of mine, to discuss concerns about tickets and fan dissatisfaction generally. Scouting director Rudy Terrasas was relieved of his duties; while I took no pleasure from a man losing his job, seeing Mets drafts in more capable hands would be key to a farm-system renaissance. Alderson also confirmed during an interview with Mets Hot Stove that he planned to go over slot on draft picks. He answered questions directly, letting the interviewer (and, by extension, the fans) know exactly why he made decisions. Always, the balance between short-term gain and long-term planning guided him; he made that connection explicit.

One of my favorite answers he gave to any question was when he explained why he'd chosen to become general manager of the Mets, a role he wouldn't have agreed to take

with most teams. After all, at sixty-two and with all the success he'd already enjoyed, Alderson easily could have pursued a
less stressful occupation. But he described the Mets as a franchise with "tremendous upside potential." And that really said
it all. As DePodesta later said in a conference call, attempting
to explain the book that made him famous, "*Moneyball* doesn't
have anything to do with on-base percentage or statistics. It's a
constant investigation of stagnant systems, to see if you can
find value where it isn't readily apparent."

What were the Mets, if not baseball's greatest market ineffi-
ciency? A New York market to draw on financially, a rabid fan
base, a brand-new stadium, and two world championships in a
half century? Of course DePodesta wanted in as Vice President
of Player Personnel and Amateur Scouting, and J.P. Ricciardi
left another job to become Special Assistant to the General Manager. This was the *Moneyball* of franchises.

I happily abdicated to them the responsibility for exploiting
every advantage inherent to the New York Mets. Sure, past
success was no guarantee of future results, as any mutual fund
will tell you. But for the first time since I could remember, I had
confidence in the group making baseball decisions about the
New York Mets. Had I gotten the job, I'd have had confidence
as well—but also a monumental undertaking and zero spare
time. Writing, a passion of mine, would have become impossible. And I'd have spent far less time with Rachel and Mirabelle
than I could possibly imagine. Instead, thanks to my current vocation, I had the opportunity to raise Mirabelle daily, to sit her
on my lap, noon on a Wednesday, to watch a baseball game from
my childhood.

It had been, as I wrote in my concession speech, Jon Niese
since the Mets had won a championship. By that I meant that

Jon Niese was born on October 27, 1986, the day the Mets won Game 7 of the 1986 World Series. A man had been born, experienced an entire childhood, signed with the Mets, played at every level in the team's minor-league system, and established himself as a rotation stalwart with a major-league team since the Mets last won a World Series. I thought about what the next twenty-four years would bring Mirabelle as I settled her on my lap, the final few innings of Game 7 playing on my DVD player. The voice of Vin Scully, which I assumed Mirabelle recognized from the womb, called the action. When Marty Barrett struck out, Jesse Orosco threw his glove high into the air, a starter's pistol for the pileup of bodies on the pitcher's mound. I did the same with Mirabelle—being far more careful than Orosco to make sure I caught the thrown object—and she started laughing, joyful at getting to spend a little time playing with me. For the first time I could remember, it was easy to imagine doing the same thing with her at Citi Field, after her generation's Orosco threw a future season's final pitch.

ACKNOWLEDGMENTS

I'd like to thank the following people for making this project such a pleasure for me.

My mother, Myrna Megdal, imbued me with the confidence to always pursue my passions and the sense of humor to enjoy them along the way. Truly, losing the race for GM is a blessing, as now I can call her more often.

To my father, Ira Megdal, who gave me the gift of baseball and books from my earliest days—I'll share both with you forever.

To my high-powered superagent, Sydelle Kramer—Sydelle, truly, I never knew it could be like this. I really enjoy getting reply e-mails from you at 2 A.M. When you are on vacation.

To my editor, Benjamin Adams, who made this book immeasurably better, while engaging in serious conversations about Roberto Petagine. Seriously. More than one. Best editing process ever. Bloomsbury has been a dream to work with, and I would be remiss not to thank George Gibson for believing in my project, and Mike O'Connor for helping to polish the book properly. They are all tremendous baseball fans, and, therefore, perfect stewards for this book.

To all my delegates, but particularly the lovely and talented

Zoë Rice, who gave me feedback throughout the process, Dan Symborski, who will make a fantastic GM candidate himself someday, and Mike Silva, a true friend who I will happily defend on Twitter for the next one hundred years.

To the Mets fans I had the opportunity to meet during the course of this campaign—not only were the conversations enjoyable, I am certain they have helped to inform my writing as well.

To Calvin Trillin, whose career taught me it is possible to write serious analysis, humor as well as rhymed verse, and whose campaign to make Spaghetti Carbonara the national Thanksgiving dish was Al Smith to my JFK.

To Deb and Ean Bauer, living proof that true friends and wonderful people can still choose to root for the New York Yankees.

To Chris Pummer, someone I've never met in person yet consider a close friend for the better part of a decade, and who built the Megdal for GM Web site in his spare time: That he has two children and full-time work makes the concept of spare time laughable, however.

To Lauren Krueger, who has been my cousin for years, and a talented filmmaker for almost as long. For the love of God, people, hire her—you won't be sorry. Her work is incredible.

To Akie Bermiss, fantastic jazz musician and composer, creator of Megdal for GM campaign soundtrack, and friend since college. It never gets old working with you on any project.

To the New York Mets—not just Deep Swoboda, but everyone who has ever played with, managed, general managed, or owned that team. Whatever my issues with you through the years, that you merely exist is cause for thanks.

To my daughter, Mirabelle: Even if you end up hating

baseball, I'll share whatever your PASSION is, as long as you'll have me.

To my wife Rachel, who has the patience of Job and the looks of Job's unattainable fantasy: No matter what people think of me, when they meet you, they know I must have something going for me, because you agreed to marry me.

A NOTE ON THE AUTHOR

HOWARD MEGDAL is the editor and creator of the Perpetual Post. He writes for Capital New York, MLBTradeRumors.com, New York Baseball Digest, and he is the poet laureate of SB Nation New York. He has written for ESPN.com, the *New York Times*, and many other publications. He lives in Rockland County, New York, with his wife, daughter, and an organizational depth chart of the Mets on the wall. His Web site is www.howardmegdal.com.